go big
Go Bold

Large-Scale Modern Quilts

Barbara Cain

10 Projects • Quick to Cut • Fast to Sew

stashBOOKS.

an imprint of C&T Publishing

Text copyright © 2015 by Barbara Cain

Photography and artwork copyright © 2015 by C&T Publishing, Inc.

PUBLISHER: Amy Marson

CREATIVE DIRECTOR: Gailen Runge

ART DIRECTOR: Kristy Zacharias

EDITOR: Lynn Koolish

TECHNICAL EDITORS: Ellen Pahl and Debbie Rodgers

COVER DESIGNER: April Mostek

BOOK DESIGNER: Christina Jarumay Fox

PRODUCTION COORDINATOR: Freesia Pearson Blizard

PRODUCTION EDITOR: Joanna Burgarino

ILLUSTRATOR: Jenny Davis

PHOTO ASSISTANT: Mary Peyton Peppo

Style photography by Nissa Brehmer and instructional photography by Diane Pedersen, unless otherwise noted

Published by Stash Books, an imprint of C&T Publishing, Inc., P.O. Box 1456, Lafayette, CA 94549

Library of Congress Cataloging-in-Publication Data

Cain, Barbara, 1960-

 Go big, go bold, large-scale modern quilts : 10 projects--quick to cut--fast to sew / Barbara Cain.

   pages cm

 ISBN 978-1-61745-087-7 (soft cover)

 1. Patchwork quilts--Patterns. I. Title.

 TT835.C34 2015

 746.46--dc23

                       2015008955

Printed in China

10 9 8 7 6 5 4 3 2 1

Dedication

This book is dedicated to my mother, Helen Summers, who was so thoughtful when planting the sewing seed in me many years ago.

Acknowledgments

Many thanks to the following manufacturers who kindly provided many of the materials used for the projects in this book: Andover Fabrics, Coats and Clark, Michael Miller Fabrics, Riley Blake Designs, Robert Kaufman Fabrics, The Warm Company, and Westminster Fibers / Lifestyle Fabrics.

A very special thank-you to my husband, John Cain, for his continuing patience, encouragement, and support of anything I get myself into.

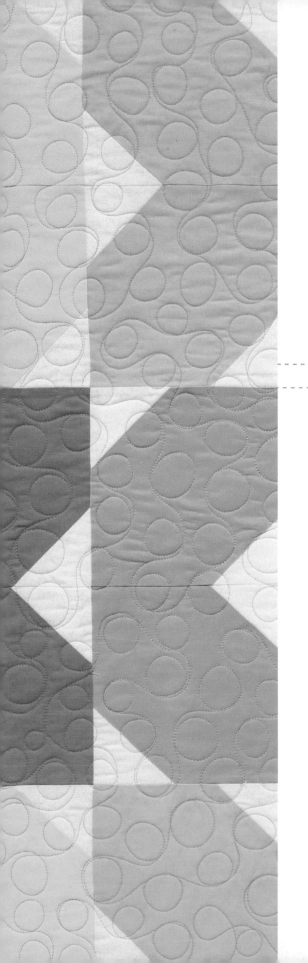

Contents

Introduction

Ask 100 quilters to define "modern quilting" and you'll get 100 different answers, the majority of them relating to the final product—improvisational, asymmetrical, bold, minimalist, borderless, just to name a few. While modern quilting is certainly about what the quilts look like, it's just as much about the process of quilting. For me, modern quilting is about using modern tools, techniques, and computer technology for learning, collaborating, and acquiring materials. It's about making efficient use of what little spare time we have to indulge ourselves in our favorite activity. Modern quilting is about the modernization of a traditional craft to make it more compatible with our contemporary lifestyles.

Whether you've just begun to make quilts or you are very experienced, you are a quilter who is living in today's busy society. Along with that, you have a few conditions that need to be met:

- You want to make the best use of the time you have available for quilting.
- You want to enjoy the process of making a quilt.
- You want to finish your quilt sooner rather than later.
- You want a quilt that is worthy of your efforts.

This book will allow you to meet those needs by teaching you to easily make bold graphic quilts for you, your family, and your friends to enjoy. The pattern pieces are much larger than their traditional counterparts, so they are quick to cut and quick to sew together. They provide the perfect spaces to showcase your favorite fabrics and quilting designs. As a bonus, the quilts have pieced backings that also exhibit big, bold character. Each backing displays a graphic pieced strip that echoes the quilt top and is flanked with a coordinating print fabric. This lets you feature either side; making these quilts essentially reversible. Choose your favorite side— you'll have two quilts in one!

Let's get started. Be bold!

—*Barbara Cain*

P. S. If you are a beginning quiltmaker, take a look at Quiltmaking Basics (page 95) and the Glossary (page 108)—these sections will provide all the information you need to make the quilts in this book.

Helpful Tips
and Techniques

Staying Organized

The fabrics for each project are numbered to make it easier for you to use the color palette of your choice. To keep organized while you are working, make a fabric numbering reference sheet for each quilt that you make. Cut a snippet from each fabric, staple the snippets to a sheet of paper, and label each accordingly. This reference will help you in quickly identifying each of your fabrics and will help prevent cutting and sewing errors.

Keep your cut fabric organized by labeling your cut pieces as indicated in the cutting charts. Make labels using scraps of paper and attach them with straight pins to the cut stacks of fabrics.

Woven fabrics stretch more and handle differently when cut crosswise (along the weft) than they do when cut lengthwise (along the warp). Two pieces of the same fabric can also appear slightly different when oriented perpendicular to each other. To keep your quilt looking uniform, stack squares cut from solids and nondirectional prints in the same direction and with right sides up. Use your label to denote orientation. This will help prevent you from inadvertently rotating the cuts.

Solid fabrics are included in most of the quilts shown in the book. While many solids are reversible, some are not. Labeling your cuts will also help you to ensure that you don't mistake the wrong side of a solid fabric for the right side.

Piecing the Quilt Backs

All the quilt backs for the projects in this book are pieced and will create a reversible quilt. They are also made 4″ larger than the quilt top on all four sides. The extra dimension is necessary to provide some wiggle room while basting and quilting.

After quilting and before binding, the excess is trimmed away. You'll cut the pieces for the back at the same time as the front. The cutting for both the top and back is included in each cutting chart.

Making and Using Templates

You will need to make cutting templates for the projects that are based on triangles. You can use the same templates for both the lap- and the twin-size quilts for each design.

1. Referring to the dimensions given in each project, use a ruler, square, and permanent marker to draw each of the templates onto mat board, poster board, or heavy cardboard.

2. Depending on your level of confidence with rotary-cutting tools and the thickness of the template material you are using, cut along the drawn lines with a rotary cutter, craft knife, or box cutter, along with a ruler and cutting mat. If your template material is thin enough, you can cut with scissors.

3. Trace around the template onto the right side of the appropriate fabric. Make the most efficient use of your fabric by rotating the template when tracing.

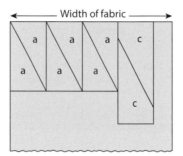

Alternate triangles for efficient use of fabric.

Note: Cutting diagrams are included for quilts made with triangles. Refer to Cutting Diagrams for Selected Quilts (page 87).

4. Place the fabric on a cutting mat and use a ruler and rotary cutter to cut along the traced lines to cut the individual pieces. For quilts that require the same cuts from 2 or more fabrics, you can cut more than one piece at a time by layering the fabrics, keeping the marked fabric on top, and then cutting through the stack. To maintain accuracy when cutting, it's best to limit the stack to 3 layers of fabric.

Working with Bias Edges

Triangles have bias-cut edges that make them vulnerable to stretching and distortion. To maintain the shape of bias-cut pieces, use spray starch and press the fabrics prior to marking and cutting. Always handle these pieces very gently when pressing, pinning, and sewing. When using starch, it's a good idea to wash the quilt after it's quilted and bound.

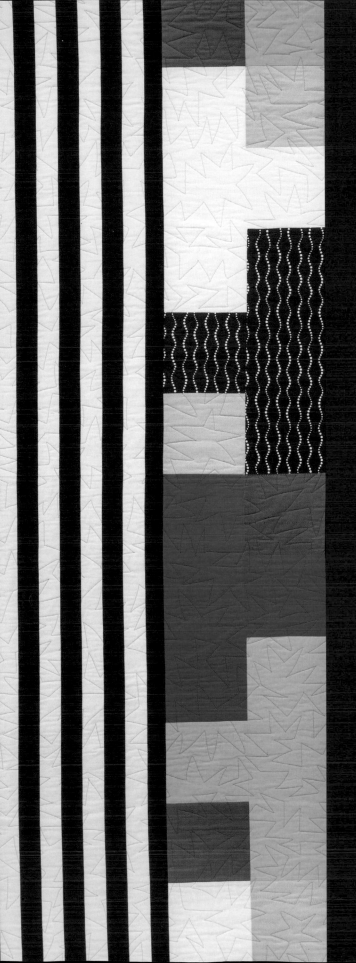

Projects

Big Blocks

Big Blocks lap-size quilt—Iceland palette, made by Barbara Cain

Finished quilts:

45″ × 60″ lap size

60″ × 90″ twin size

BLOCKS ARE THE MOST BASIC BUILDING ELEMENT. THEY ARE SO PLAIN IN CHARACTER YET SO FULL OF POTENTIAL. FOR *BIG BLOCKS*, THESE SIMPLE SHAPES COME TOGETHER AND FORM AN EASILY CONSTRUCTED BUT COMPLEX-LOOKING DESIGN.

Fabrics

The secret to a successful *Big Blocks* quilt is to use six fabrics that vary in value from very light to very dark, so there is strong contrast. Solids and prints are both fine to use; however, when choosing prints, consider their scale, and avoid directional prints. Small-scale prints will allow the size and shape of the blocks to remain center stage; larger-scale or directional prints would be distracting.

The quilt back is made of a block feature section that is constructed the same way as the quilt top. The feature section is flanked by two fabric panels that look great when made with large-scale prints.

Choose your palette for *Big Blocks* from the Palette Suggestions (page 14), or better yet, make up your own palette, one that is reflective of you. Do you like things spicy or are you calm and reserved? Do you like the beach or is a skiing vacation more your style? The possibilities are endless. Express yourself in your quilt!

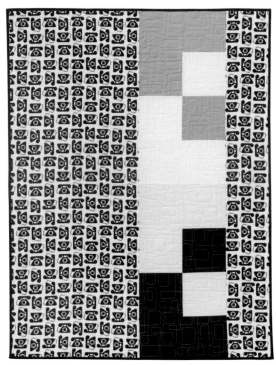

Big Blocks lap-size quilt back

MATERIALS

Yardages are based on 40″-wide fabric.

Material	Description	Lap quilt (45″ × 60″)	Twin quilt (60″ × 90″)
Fabric 1	White solid for the blocks	¾ yard	1 yard
Fabric 2	Black solid for the blocks	⅞ yard	1¼ yards
Fabric 3	Pale turquoise for the blocks	¾ yard	1 yard
Fabric 4	Medium turquoise for the blocks	⅞ yard	1 yard
Fabric 5	Pale green for the blocks	⅝ yard	1¼ yards
Fabric 6	Medium green for the blocks	⅝ yard	1 yard
Fabric 7	Black-and-white print for the back panels	2 yards	4¼ yards*
Fabric 8	Black solid for the binding	½ yard	¾ yard
Batting		53″ × 68″	68″ × 98″

* The narrower back panel requires piecing. To avoid piecing, you'll need 5⅝ yards.

CUTTING

Refer to Staying Organized (page 5) for tips on keeping track of your cut fabric.

When subcutting strips, cut the longest pieces first.

Material	Lap quilt (45″ × 60″)	Twin quilt (60″ × 90″)

Fabric 1	Cut 3 strips 8″ × width of fabric; subcut into:
	  6 squares 8″ × 8″ (1a)
	  3 rectangles 8″ × 15½″ (1b)
		Cut 2 strips 8″ × width of fabric; subcut into:
		  10 squares 8″ × 8″ (1a)
		Cut 1 strip 15½″ × width of fabric; subcut into:
		  5 rectangles 8″ × 15½″ (1b)

Fabric 2	Cut 3 strips 8″ × width of fabric; subcut into:
	  5 squares 8″ × 8″ (2a)
	  2 rectangles 8″ × 15½″ (2b)
	  1 rectangle 8″ × 19¼″ (2c)
	  1 rectangle 8″ × 11¾″ (2d)
		Cut 5 strips 8″ × width of fabric; subcut into:
		  9 squares 8″ × 8″ (2a)
		  4 rectangles 8″ × 15½″ (2b)
		  1 rectangle 8″ × 19¼″ (2c)
		  1 rectangle 8″ × 11¾″ (2d)

Fabric 3	Cut 3 strips 8″ × width of fabric; subcut into:
	  6 squares 8″ × 8″ (3a)
	  3 rectangles 8″ × 15½″ (3b)
		Cut 2 strips 8″ × width of fabric; subcut into:
		  10 squares 8″ × 8″ (3a)
		Cut 1 strip 15½″ × width of fabric; subcut into:
		  5 rectangles 8″ × 15½″ (3b)

Fabric 4	Cut 3 strips 8″ × width of fabric; subcut into:
	  5 squares 8″ × 8″ (4a)
	  2 rectangles 8″ × 15½″ (4b)
	  1 rectangle 8″ × 19¼″ (4c)
	  1 rectangle 8″ × 11¾″ (4d)
		Cut 2 strips 8″ × width of fabric; subcut into:
		  10 squares 8″ × 8″ (4a)
		Cut 1 strip 15½″ × width of fabric; subcut into:
		  5 rectangles 8″ × 15½″ (4b)

Fabric 5	Cut 2 strips 8″ × width of fabric; subcut into:
	  4 squares 8″ × 8″ (5a)
	  2 rectangles 8″ × 15½″ (5b)
		Cut 5 strips 8″ × width of fabric; subcut into:
		  9 squares 8″ × 8″ (5a)
		  4 rectangles 8″ × 15½″ (5b)
		  1 rectangle 8″ × 19¼″ (5c)
		  1 rectangle 8″ × 11¾″ (5d)

Fabric 6	Cut 2 strips 8″ × width of fabric; subcut into:
	  4 squares 8″ × 8″ (6a)
	  2 rectangles 8″ × 15½″ (6b)
		Cut 2 strips 8″ × width of fabric; subcut into:
		  10 squares 8″ × 8″ (6a)
		Cut 1 strip 15½″ × width of fabric; subcut into:
		  5 rectangles 8″ × 15½″ (6b)

Fabric 7	Cut 1 piece 26¾″ × 68″ (7e) Cut 1 piece 11¾″ × 68″ (7f)	Cut 1 piece 34¼″ × 98″ (7g) Cut 2 pieces 19¼″ × 49¼″ (7h)*
Fabric 8	Cut 6 strips 2½″ × width of fabric for binding	Cut 9 strips 2½″ × width of fabric for binding

* Carefully cut the fabric so that the print will match when the pieces are joined. OR if you have 5⅝ yards, cut 1 piece 19¼″ × 98″ (7h).

Construction

Big Blocks is assembled in columns. All seam allowances are ¼˝ and are pressed to one side. For odd-numbered columns, press the seams in one direction; for even-numbered columns, press the seams in the opposite direction. Between columns, press all the seams in one direction.

QUILT TOP

Refer to either the lap-size quilt assembly diagram or the twin-size quilt assembly diagram.

1. Sew together the pieces into pairs and press.

2. Sew together the pairs into columns and press.

3. Sew together the columns to assemble the quilt top and press.

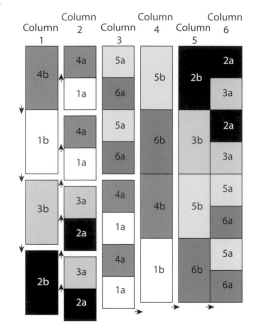

Lap-size quilt assembly

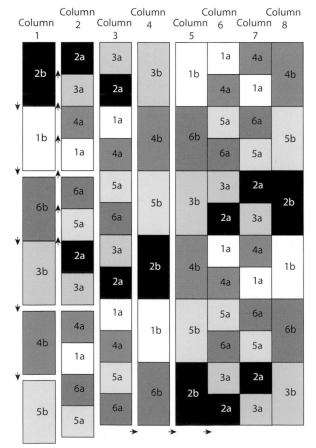

Twin-size quilt assembly

QUILT BACK

Refer to either the lap-size quilt back assembly diagram or the twin-size quilt back assembly diagram.

1. Sew together the pieces into pairs and press. Note: If you are piecing the back panel for the twin-size quilt, match the print pattern of the 7h pieces.

2. Sew together the pairs into columns and press.

3. Sew together the columns to assemble the quilt back and press.

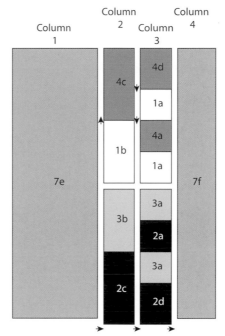

Lap-size quilt back assembly

FINISHING

Refer to Quilt Finishing (page 103) for instructions on sandwiching, basting, quilting, and binding.

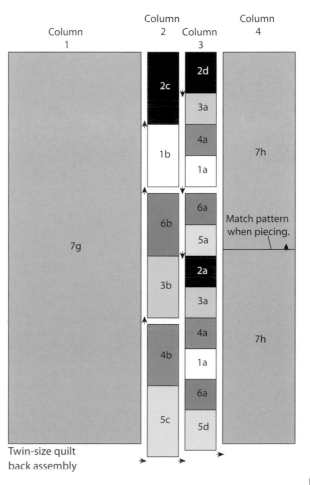

Twin-size quilt back assembly

Palette Suggestions

Below are just a few ideas for color combinations for *Big Blocks*. Looking for some punch for a boy's room? The Car Cruise palette and an accent wall with brilliant orange racing stripes would get the job done. If you would like a more sophisticated look, try a quilt in the Midnight palette. It would look great draped over a classic black leather lounge chair.

Minty

Midnight

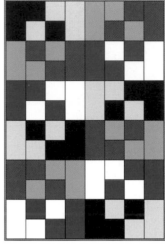

Car Cruise

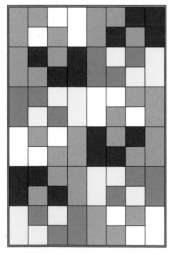

Harvest

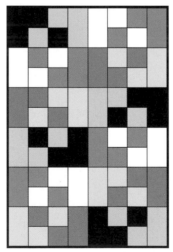

Iceland

Seashell

Big Blooms

Big Blooms lap-size quilt—Lush palette, made by Barbara Cain and Helen Summers, quilted by Barbara Cain

Finished quilts:

45″ × 60″ lap size

60″ × 90″ twin size

LIKE A BOUQUET, *BIG BLOOMS* IS PACKED WITH FLOWERS; 12 STEMS FOR THE LAP-SIZE QUILT AND 24 FOR THE TWIN SIZE. ALTHOUGH THE BLOCKS APPEAR AS IF THEY WERE MADE FROM TRIANGULAR CUTS, THEY ARE ACTUALLY MADE FROM SIMPLE SQUARES THAT ARE SEWN TOGETHER DIAGONALLY.

Fabrics

Big Blooms is made with two colors of flower blocks, each with three parts: petals, centers, and backgrounds. Using prints for any of the flower parts is fine, but be sure that the prints are nondirectional and small in scale so that they don't compete with the size and shape of the flowers. Also, be sure to use fabrics that contrast with each other so that each flower shape stands out, rather than blending into the background.

The quilt back is made of a blooms feature section that is constructed the same way as the quilt top. Fabric panels are added to this section in order to complete the back.

The *Big Blooms* quilt top featured in this project is made from both solid and print fabrics in the Lush palette, but you can choose your palette to match the colors to your favorite flower and have a year-round bouquet. You can also make a choice from the Palette Suggestions (page 23).

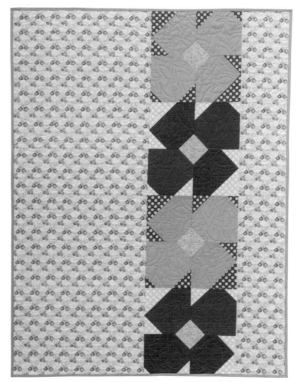

Big Blooms lap-size quilt back

MATERIALS

Yardages are based on 40"-wide fabric.

Material	Description	Lap quilt (45" × 60")	Twin quilt (60" × 90")
Fabric 1	Light violet solid for the light petals	1¾ yards	3 yards
Fabric 2	Dark violet solid for the dark petals	1¾ yards	3 yards
Fabric 3	Medium turquoise print for the flower centers	⅝ yard	1 yard
Fabric 4	Dark green print for the dark backgrounds	1 yard	1⅝ yards
Fabric 5	Light green print for the light backgrounds	1 yard	1⅝ yards
Fabric 6	Multicolored print for the back panels	2 yards	4¼ yards*
Fabric 7	Light violet solid for the binding	½ yard	¾ yard
Batting		53" × 68"	68" × 98"

* The narrower back panel requires piecing. To avoid piecing, you'll need 5⅝ yards.

CUTTING

Refer to Staying Organized (page 5) for tips on keeping track of your cut fabric.

When subcutting strips, cut the longest pieces first.

Material	Lap quilt (45˝ × 60˝)	Twin quilt (60˝ × 90˝)
Fabric 1	Cut 7 strips 8˝ × width of fabric; subcut into: 30 squares 8˝ × 8˝ (1a) 2 rectangles 8˝ × 11¾˝ (1b)	Cut 13 strips 8˝ × width of fabric; subcut into: 58 squares 8˝ × 8˝ (1a) 2 rectangles 8˝ × 11¾˝ (1b)
Fabric 2	Cut 7 strips 8˝ × width of fabric; subcut into: 30 squares 8˝ × 8˝ (2a) 2 rectangles 8˝ × 11¾˝ (2b)	Cut 13 strips 8˝ × width of fabric; subcut into: 58 squares 8˝ × 8˝ (2a) 2 rectangles 8˝ × 11¾˝ (2b)
Fabric 3	Cut 5 strips 3˝ × width of fabric; subcut into: 64 squares 3˝ × 3˝ (3c)	Cut 10 strips 3˝ × width of fabric; subcut into: 120 squares 3˝ × 3˝ (3c)
Fabric 4	Cut 2 strips 5˝ × width of fabric; subcut into: 15 squares 5˝ × 5˝ (4d) Cut 3 strips 3½˝ × width of fabric; subcut into: 31 squares 3½˝ × 3½˝ (4e) Cut 1 strip 2½˝ × width of fabric; subcut into: 15 squares 2½˝ × 2½˝ (4f) Cut 1 strip 9˝ × width of fabric; subcut into: 1 square 9˝ × 9˝ (4g) 1 square 7½˝ × 7½˝ (4h) 1 square 6½˝ × 6½˝ (4i)	Cut 4 strips 5˝ × width of fabric; subcut into: 29 squares 5˝ × 5˝ (4d) 4 squares 3½˝ × 3½˝ (4e) Cut 5 strips 3½˝ × width of fabric; subcut into: 55 squares 3½˝ × 3½˝ (4e) Cut 2 strips 2½˝ × width of fabric; subcut into: 29 squares 2½˝ × 2½˝ (4f) Cut 1 strip 9˝ × width of fabric; subcut into: 1 square 9˝ × 9˝ (4g) 1 square 7½˝ × 7½˝ (4h) 1 square 6½˝ × 6½˝ (4i)
Fabric 5	Cut 2 strips 5˝ × width of fabric; subcut into: 15 squares 5˝ × 5˝ (5d) Cut 3 strips 3½˝ × width of fabric; subcut into: 31 squares 3½˝ × 3½˝ (5e) Cut 1 strip 2½˝ × width of fabric; subcut into: 15 squares 2½˝ × 2½˝ (5f) Cut 1 strip 9˝ × width of fabric; subcut into: 1 square 9˝ × 9˝ (5g) 1 square 7½˝ × 7½˝ (5h) 1 square 6½˝ × 6½˝ (5i)	Cut 4 strips 5˝ × width of fabric; subcut into: 29 squares 5˝ × 5˝ (5d) 4 squares 3½˝ × 3½˝ (5e) Cut 5 strips 3½˝ × width of fabric; subcut into: 55 squares 3½˝ × 3½˝ (5e) Cut 2 strips 2½˝ × width of fabric; subcut into: 29 squares 2½˝ × 2½˝ (5f) Cut 1 strip 9˝ × width of fabric; subcut into: 1 square 9˝ × 9˝ (5g) 1 square 7½˝ × 7½˝ (5h) 1 square 6½˝ × 6½˝ (5i)
Fabric 6	Cut 1 piece 26¾˝ × 68˝ (6j) Cut 1 piece 11¾˝ × 68˝ (6k)	Cut 1 piece 34¼˝ × 98˝ (6l) Cut 2 pieces 19¼˝ × 49¼˝ (6m)*
Fabric 7	Cut 6 strips 2½˝ × width of fabric for binding	Cut 9 strips 2½˝ × width of fabric for binding

* Carefully cut the fabric so that the print will match when the pieces are joined. OR if you have 5⅝ yards, cut 1 piece 19¼˝ × 98˝ (6m).

Preparation

On the wrong side of each flower center and background square (Fabrics 3, 4, and 5), draw a diagonal stitching line from one corner to the opposite corner. If you are using directional prints, do a quick check to make sure that the print will be oriented correctly when sewn. If not, draw the diagonal line between the opposite two corners.

Construction

Big Blooms is assembled in quarter-blocks or quadrants that are assembled into rows that form the quilt top. For the quilt back, the quadrants are assembled into columns. All seam allowances are ¼″ and are pressed to one side. To emphasize the blooms, press the seam allowances toward the petal fabric, with the exception of the flower centers. For those, follow the arrows in the diagrams for pressing direction. When sewing the quadrants together in rows, press the seams of odd-numbered rows in one direction, and press the seams of even-numbered rows in the opposite direction. After joining the rows, press all of the seams in one direction.

QUADRANTS

1. With right sides together, pin the flower center and background pieces onto the petal pieces as shown. Sew along the diagonal lines. Trim off the corners ¼″ away from the sewing lines and press in the direction of the arrows.

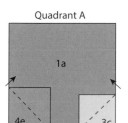

Quadrant A

Lap size: Make 15.
Twin size: Make 29.

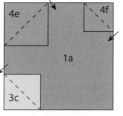

Quadrant B

Lap size: Make 15.
Twin size: Make 29.

Quadrant C

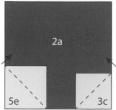

2a

5e   3c

Lap size: Make 15.
Twin size: Make 29.

Quadrant D

5e   5f

2a

3c

Lap size: Make 15.
Twin size: Make 29.

Quadrant E

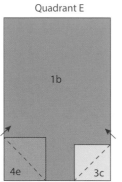

1b

4e   3c

Lap size: Make 1.
Twin size: Make 1.

Quadrant F

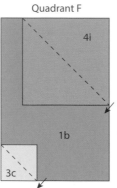

4i

1b

3c

Lap size: Make 1.
Twin size: Make 1.

Quadrant G

2b

5e   3c

Lap size: Make 1.
Twin size: Make 1.

Quadrant H

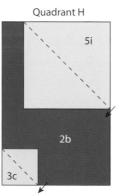

5i

2b

3c

Lap size: Make 1.
Twin size: Make 1.

2. With right sides together, pin the remaining background pieces onto the partially complete quadrants. Sew along the diagonal lines.

Quadrant A

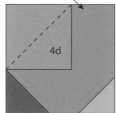

4d

Lap size: Make 15.
Twin size: Make 29.

Quadrant C

5d

Lap size: Make 15.
Twin size: Make 29.

Quadrant E

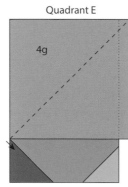

4g

Lap size: Make 1.
Twin size: Make 1.

Quadrant F

4h

Lap size: Make 1.
Twin size: Make 1.

Quadrant G

5g

Lap size: Make 1.
Twin size: Make 1.

Quadrant H

5h

Lap size: Make 1.
Twin size: Make 1.

3. Trim off the corners ¼" away from the sewing lines and press. Trim off the protruding dog-ears from quadrants E and G.

- -

Salvaging Scraps

If you like working with scraps, save the trimmings for another project. There will be enough to make a throw pillow or small quilt.

- -

QUILT TOP

Refer to either the lap-size quilt assembly diagram or the twin-size quilt assembly diagram.

1. Arrange the quadrants in rows, rotating them as needed. Sew together the quadrants into pairs and press.

2. Sew together the pairs into rows and press.

3. Sew together the rows to assemble the quilt top and press.

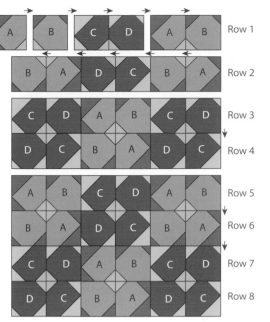

Lap-size quilt assembly

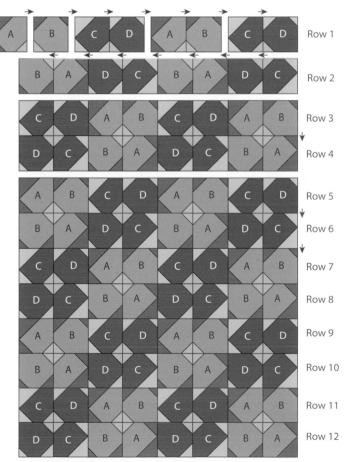

Twin-size quilt assembly

QUILT BACK

Refer to either the lap-size quilt back assembly diagram or the twin-size quilt back assembly diagram.

1. Sew together the quadrants into pairs and press. Note: If you are piecing the back panel for the twin-size quilt, match the print pattern of the 6m pieces.

2. Sew together the pairs into columns and press.

3. Sew together the columns to assemble the quilt back and press.

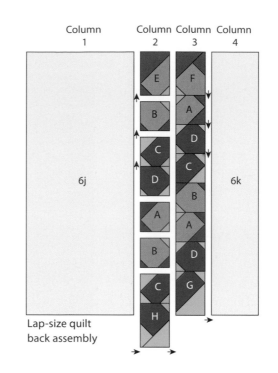

Lap-size quilt back assembly

FINISHING

Refer to Quilt Finishing (page 103) for instructions on sandwiching, basting, quilting, and binding.

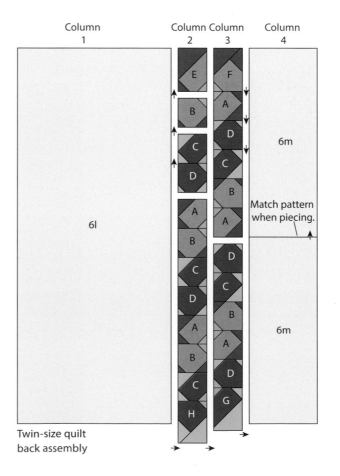

Twin-size quilt back assembly

Palette Suggestions

You can make any flower you like just by changing the petal fabric.
The October palette could be lilies, gerbera daisies, or mums, while the
Blush palette looks a bit more like cherry blossoms or tulips. For a great
Saint Valentine's Day gift, the Roses palette would be just perfect.

Blush

October

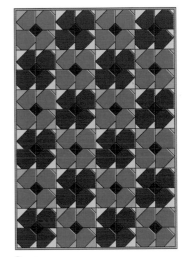

Roses

Classic

Sea

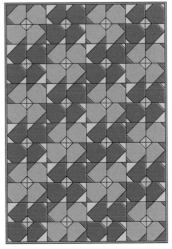

Lush

Big Harlequin

Big Harlequin lap size quilt—Princess palette, made by Barbara Cain

Finished quilts:

45″ × 60″ lap size

60″ × 90″ twin size

THE HARLEQUIN PATTERN IS NAMED AFTER A LIVELY SIXTEENTH-CENTURY ITALIAN COMEDIC CHARACTER WHO DRESSED IN BRIGHTLY COLORED, DIAMOND-PATTERNED CLOTHING. THIS QUILT HAS ALL OF HARLEQUIN'S AMUSING PERSONALITY WITH ITS BIG BOLD DIAMONDS AND HUGE OPPORTUNITIES FOR COLOR PLAY.

Fabrics

The *Big Harlequin* quilt top is made with four colorful feature fabrics and two neutral background fabrics. To make the diamonds really stand out, make sure there is plenty of contrast between all the fabrics.

The quilt back is made of a harlequin feature section that is constructed the same way as the quilt top. Fabric panels flank the feature section and complete the back. The panels are sizable and provide a great opportunity to use a large-scale print.

As shown, the *Big Harlequin* quilt top is made from solid fabrics in the Princess palette. This quilt is all girl and screams for some pink plush pillows and gold glitter accessories. If you'd like something a bit less feminine, check out the Palette Suggestions (page 31).

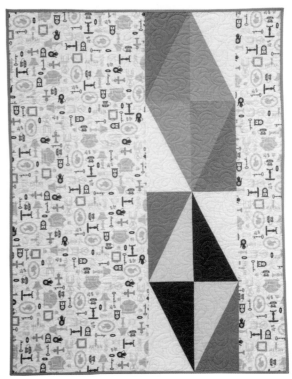

Big Harlequin lap-size quilt back

MATERIALS

Yardages are based on 40˝-wide fabric.

Material	Description	Lap quilt (45˝ × 60˝)	Twin quilt (60˝ × 90˝)
Fabric 1	Mushroom solid for the background triangles	1¼ yards	2 yards
Fabric 2	Bone solid for the background triangles	1¼ yards	2 yards
Fabric 3	Light pink solid for the feature triangles	½ yard	1 yard
Fabric 4	Dark pink solid for the feature triangles	½ yard	1 yard
Fabric 5	Caramel solid for the feature triangles	½ yard	1 yard
Fabric 6	Dark brown solid for the feature triangles	½ yard	1 yard
Fabric 7	Multicolored print for the back panels	2 yards	4¼ yards*
Fabric 8	Caramel solid for the binding	½ yard	¾ yard
Batting		53˝ × 68˝	68˝ × 98˝
Template material	Mat board, poster board, or heavy cardboard	18˝ × 22˝	18˝ × 22˝

* The narrower back panel requires piecing. To avoid piecing, you'll need 5⅝ yards.

CUTTING

Refer to Staying Organized (page 5) for tips on keeping track of your cut fabric.

Refer to Cutting Diagrams for Selected Quilts (page 87).

Important! Starch your fabric before cutting triangles. Refer to Working with Bias Edges (page 6).

Material	Lap quilt (45″ × 60″)	Twin quilt (60″ × 90″)
Fabric 1	Cut 14 b triangles (1b) Cut 2 d extended triangles (1d)	Cut 28 b triangles (1b) Cut 2 d extended triangles (1d)
Fabric 2	Cut 14 a triangles (2a) Cut 2 c extended triangles (2c)	Cut 28 a triangles (2a) Cut 2 c extended triangles (2c)
Fabric 3	Cut 8 b triangles (3b)	Cut 14 b triangles (3b)
Fabric 4	Cut 8 a triangles (4a)	Cut 16 a triangles (4a)
Fabric 5	Cut 8 b triangles (5b)	Cut 16 b triangles (5b)
Fabric 6	Cut 8 a triangles (6a)	Cut 14 a triangles (6a)
Fabric 7	Cut 1 piece 26¾″ × 68″ (7e) Cut 1 piece 11¾″ × 68″ (7f)	Cut 1 piece 34¼″ × 98″ (7g) Cut 2 pieces 19¼″ × 49¼″ (7h)*
Fabric 8	Cut 6 strips 2½″ × width of fabric for binding	Cut 9 strips 2½″ × width of fabric for binding

* Carefully cut the fabric so that the print will match when the pieces are joined. OR if you have 5⅜ yards, cut 1 piece 19¼″ × 98″ (7h).

Make Templates

Refer to Making and Using Templates (page 6).

Make an a/b triangle and an extended c/d triangle as shown.

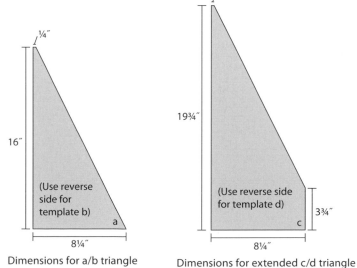

Dimensions for a/b triangle

Dimensions for extended c/d triangle

Construction

Big Harlequin is assembled in triangular pairs that are further assembled into rows that form the quilt top. For the quilt back, the pairs are assembled into columns.

All seam allowances are ¼˝ and are pressed to one side. For odd-numbered rows and columns, press the seams in one direction; for even-numbered rows and columns, press the seams in the opposite direction. Between rows and columns, press all the seams in one direction.

TRIANGLE PAIRS

To ensure proper alignment of triangle pairs, carefully refer to the assembly diagrams that follow.

Triangle to Triangle

1. With right sides up, place the triangles to be paired side by side. Flip one triangle onto the other along the edge to be sewn.

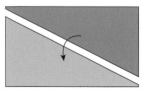

Pair triangles side by side.

2. The diagonal edges of the triangles are exactly the same size. Align these accurately, matching the outermost points of both triangles. Gently pin together the triangles.

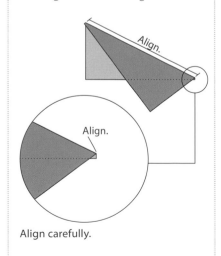

Align carefully.

3. Sew together the triangles ¼˝ away from the aligned edge.

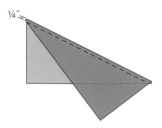

4. Open up the unit and press the seam allowance toward the darker fabric. Trim equal amounts from each end of the unit so that it is 15½˝ long.

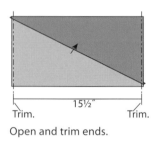

Open and trim ends.

5. Repeat Steps 1–4 to make triangle pairs in the fabric combinations as shown.

Make 7 of each for lap size; make 14 of each for twin size.

Triangle to Extended Triangle

In a manner similar to Triangle to Triangle (page 28), sew together the pieces as shown. Refer to either the lap-size quilt back assembly diagram (page 30) or the twin-size quilt back assembly diagram (page 30) for the correct fabric combinations.

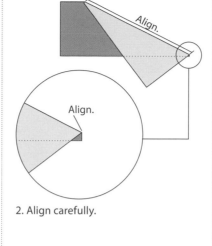

2. Align carefully.

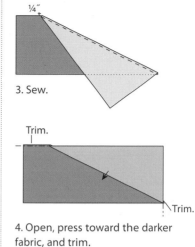

3. Sew.

4. Open, press toward the darker fabric, and trim.

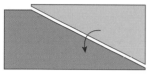

1. Pair triangles side by side.

QUILT TOP

Refer to either the lap-size quilt assembly diagram or the twin-size quilt assembly diagram.

1. Arrange the triangle pairs in rows as shown. Sew together the pieces into pairs and press.

2. Sew together the pairs into rows and press.

3. Sew together the rows to assemble the quilt top and press.

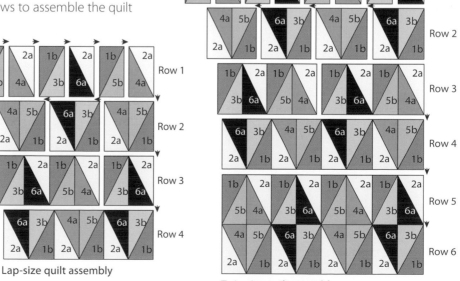

Lap-size quilt assembly

Twin-size quilt assembly

QUILT BACK

Refer to either the lap-size quilt back assembly diagram or the twin-size quilt back assembly diagram.

1. Sew together the pieces into pairs and press. Note: If you are piecing the back panel for the twin-size quilt, match the print pattern of the 7h pieces.

2. Sew together the pairs into columns and press.

3. Sew together the columns to assemble the quilt back and press.

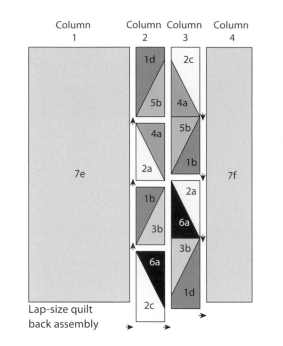

Lap-size quilt back assembly

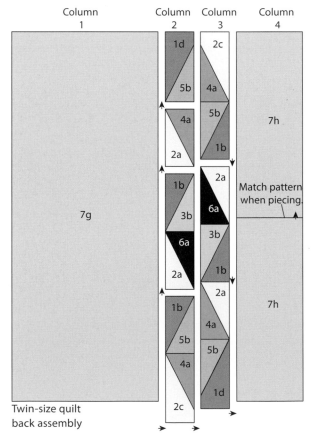

Twin-size quilt back assembly

Palette Suggestions

Big Harlequin is all about whimsy and cheer. Choose from one of these fun palettes or make your own colorful selections and show off your inner harlequin!

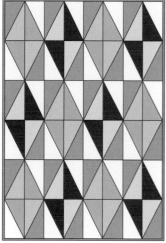

Princess

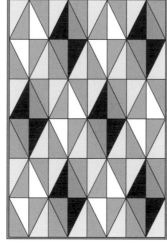

Dragon

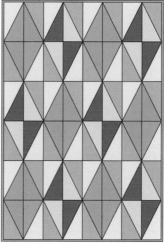

Marigold

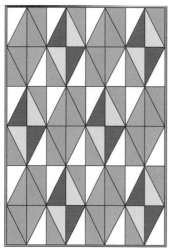

Grapes

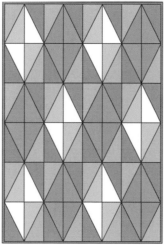

Sea Glass

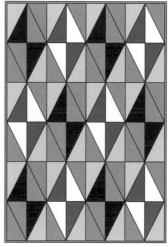

Paris

Big Isosceles

Big Isosceles twin-size quilt—Molly palette, made by Barbara Cain

Finished quilts:

45″ × 60″ lap size

60″ × 90″ twin size

BIG, 15″-WIDE ISOSCELES TRIANGLES COME TOGETHER TO MAKE THIS HIGH-IMPACT, EASY-TO-ASSEMBLE QUILT. *BIG ISOSCELES* OFFERS PLENTY OF OPPORTUNITY TO SHOWCASE YOUR FAVORITE COLORS, PRINTS, AND QUILTING IN BOTH THE TRIANGULAR PEAKS AND THE NEUTRAL VALLEYS THAT SURROUND THEM.

Fabrics

The *Big Isosceles* quilt top is made with six feature fabrics and one background fabric. Solids and prints both work great for this quilt; however, when using prints, it's best to select those that are nondirectional.

The quilt back is made using an isosceles feature section that is constructed the same way as the quilt top. Fabric panels flank the feature section to complete the back. The back panels are large enough to handle big, bold fabric selections, so don't be shy when it comes to making a choice for these.

As shown, *Big Isosceles* is made from solid fabrics in the Molly palette. Warm yellow tones peppered with two shades of salmon give this quilt an unmistakably inviting charm. Other color combinations are in Palette Suggestions (page 40).

Big Isosceles twin-size quilt back

MATERIALS

Yardages are based on 40˝-wide fabric.

Material	Description	Lap quilt (45˝ × 60˝)	Twin quilt (60˝ × 90˝)
Fabric 1	Copper solid for the feature triangles	½ yard	1⅛ yards
Fabric 2	Mango solid for the feature triangles	½ yard	1 yard
Fabric 3	Yellow solid for the feature triangles	⅔ yard	1 yard
Fabric 4	Gold solid for the feature triangles	½ yard	1 yard
Fabric 5	Salmon solid for the feature triangles	½ yard	1 yard
Fabric 6	Peach solid for the feature triangles	½ yard	1 yard
Fabric 7	White solid for the background triangles	2¼ yards	3½ yards
Fabric 8	Multicolored print for the back panels	2 yards	4¼ yards*
Fabric 9	Yellow solid for the binding	½ yard	¾ yard
Batting		53˝ × 68˝	68˝ × 98˝
Template material	Mat board, poster board, or heavy cardboard	30˝ × 36˝	30˝ × 36˝

* The narrower back panel requires piecing. To avoid piecing, you'll need 5⅝ yards.

CUTTING

Refer to Staying Organized (page 5) for tips on keeping track of your cut fabric.

Refer to Cutting Diagrams for Selected Quilts (page 87).

Important! Starch your fabric before cutting triangles. Refer to Working with Bias Edges (page 6).

Material	Lap quilt (45″ × 60″)	Twin quilt (60″ × 90″)
Fabric 1	Cut 2 a triangles (1a)	Cut 4 a triangles (1a) Cut 1 f extended triangle (1f)
Fabric 2	Cut 3 a triangles (2a)	Cut 5 a triangles (2a)
Fabric 3	Cut 2 a triangles (3a) Cut 1 f extended triangle (3f)	Cut 5 a triangles (3a)
Fabric 4	Cut 3 a triangles (4a)	Cut 5 a triangles (4a)
Fabric 5	Cut 2 a triangles (5a)	Cut 5 a triangles (5a)
Fabric 6	Cut 3 a triangles (6a)	Cut 5 a triangles (6a)

Fabric 7	Cut 2 strips 15¾″ × width of fabric; subcut into:
	    8 a triangles (7a)*
	    1 b edge triangle (7b)
	    1 c edge triangle (7c)
	 Cut 2 strips 19¼ × width of fabric; subcut into:
	    6 b edge triangles (7b)
	    6 c edge triangles (7c)
	    1 d extended edge triangle (7d)**
	    1 e extended edge triangle (7e)**
		Cut 5 strips 15¾″ × width of fabric; subcut into:
		    18 a triangles (7a)*
		    8 c edge triangles (7c)
		 Cut 1 strip 15½″ × width of fabric; subcut into:
		    6 b edge triangles (7b)
		    2 c edge triangles (7c)
		 Cut 1 strip 19¼″ × width of fabric; subcut into:
		    5 b edge triangles (7b)
		    1 c edge triangle (7c)
		    1 d extended edge triangle (7d)**
		    1 e extended edge triangle (7e)**

Fabric 8	Cut 1 piece 26¾″ × 68″ (8g) Cut 1 piece 11¾″ × 68″ (8h)	Cut 1 piece 34¼″ × 98″ (8i) Cut 2 pieces 19¼″ × 49¼″ (8j)***
Fabric 9	Cut 6 strips 2½″ × width of fabric for binding	Cut 9 strips 2½″ × width of fabric for binding

* Cut the a triangles first, and then cut c and b triangles from the remainder of the strips.

** Cut the d and e triangles first, and then cut c and b triangles from the remainder of the strips.

*** Carefully cut the fabric so that the print will match when the pieces are joined. OR if you have 5⅝ yards, cut 1 piece 19¼″ × 98″ (8j).

- -

Stacking Triangles

When stacking triangles cut from solids and nondirectional prints, it is easy to inadvertently rotate them and lose track of their orientation. To keep the triangle stacks uniform, insert a pin through the bottom or base edge to denote the orientation.

- -

Make Templates

Refer to Making and Using Templates (page 6).

Make templates for the a isosceles triangle, b/c edge triangle, d/e extended edge triangle, and f extended isosceles triangle as shown.

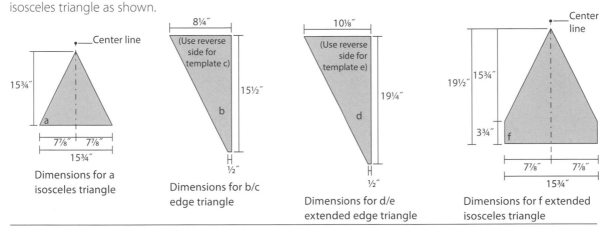

Dimensions for a isosceles triangle

Dimensions for b/c edge triangle

Dimensions for d/e extended edge triangle

Dimensions for f extended isosceles triangle

Construction

Big Isosceles is assembled in triangular pairs that are further assembled into rows that form the quilt top. For the quilt back, the triangles are assembled into blocks and then into columns. All seam allowances are ¼″ and are pressed to one side. It may be easiest to wait until the pairs are arranged in rows before pressing. Or you can assemble one row at a time when sewing triangles together in pairs. For odd-numbered rows, press the seams in one direction; for even-numbered rows, press the seams in the opposite direction. After joining the rows, press all the seams in one direction.

TRIANGLE PAIRS

To ensure proper alignment of triangle pairs, refer to the assembly diagrams that follow.

Triangle to Triangle

1. With right sides up, place the triangles to be paired side by side. Flip one triangle onto the other along the edge to be sewn.

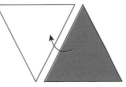

Pair triangles side by side.

2. Keeping the edges to be sewn aligned, slightly shift the pieces so that the lower isosceles triangle extends beyond the upper, until the lower triangle, the upper triangle, and the ¼″ seamline all intersect at the same point. Gently pin and sew together the pieces using a ¼″ seam.

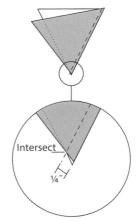

Intersect

¼″

Align, shift, and sew.

Edge Triangle to Triangle

In a manner similar to Triangle to Triangle (page 36), sew together the pieces as shown.

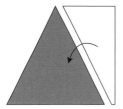

1. Pair triangles side by side.

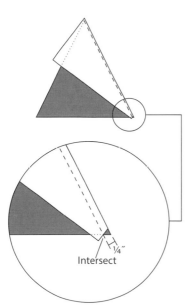

2. Align, shift, and sew.

Extended Edge Triangle to Triangle

1. With right sides up, place a 6a isosceles triangle and a 7d extended edge triangle side by side. Flip 7d onto 6a along the edge to be sewn.

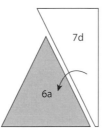

Pair triangles side by side.

2. Keeping the edges to be sewn aligned, slightly shift the pieces so that 6a extends beyond 7d, until 6a, 7d, and the ¼″ seamline all intersect at the same point. Gently pin and sew together the pieces using a ¼″ seam.

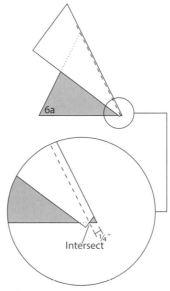

Align, shift, and sew.

3. Open up the unit and press the seam allowance to the side. Trim 7d to align with 6a as indicated.

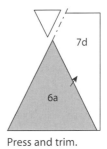

Press and trim.

4. Repeat Steps 1 and 2 to add piece 7e extended edge triangle to the 6a/7d unit. Open up the unit and press.

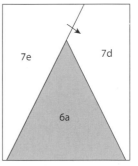

Sew and press.

QUILT TOP

Refer to either the lap-size quilt assembly diagram or the twin-size quilt assembly diagram.

1. Sew together the pieces into pairs and press.

2. Sew the pairs into rows. If any stretching has occurred, trim the rows to a height of 15½″. This consists of 15¼″ from the center of the triangle base to its opposite point, plus a ¼″ seam allowance from the point to the edge of the row.

3. Sew together the rows to assemble the quilt top and press.

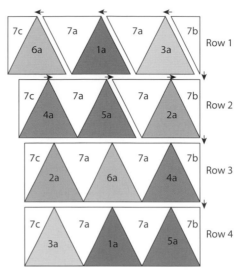

Lap-size quilt top assembly

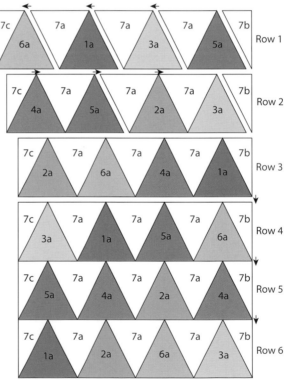

Twin-size quilt top assembly

QUILT BACK

Refer to either the lap-size quilt back assembly diagram or the twin-size quilt back assembly diagram.

1. Sew together the triangles to make the blocks, as shown, and press. Note: If you are piecing the back panel for the twin-size quilt, match the print pattern of the 8j pieces.

2. Sew together the blocks into a column and press.

3. Sew together the columns to assemble the quilt back and press.

FINISHING

Refer to Quilt Finishing (page 103) for instructions on sandwiching, basting, quilting, and binding.

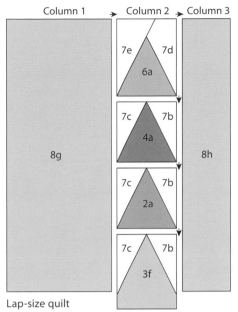

Lap-size quilt back assembly

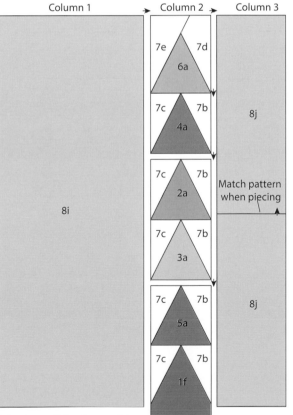

Twin-size quilt back assembly

Palette Suggestions

Big Isosceles can have a brilliant, subtle, modern, or traditional appearance, all depending on the fabric selection. The Speedy and Caution palettes are very lively and would make great quilts for energetic teenage boys. If you want something subtler, the Pastel and Antique palettes are both very soothing. Take your pick or create a palette of your own.

Speedy

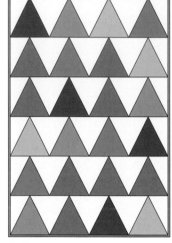

Max

Antique

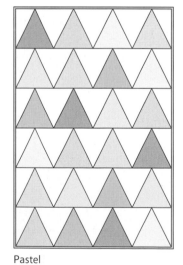

Pastel

Caution

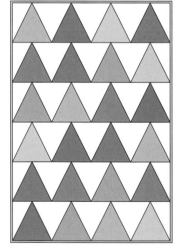

Molly

Big Love

Big Love lap-size quilt—Bahamas palette, made by Barbara Cain and Helen Summers, quilted by Barbara Cain

Finished quilts:

45″ × 60″ lap size

60″ × 90″ twin size

BOLD X'S AND O'S HUG AND KISS ONE ANOTHER TO MAKE THIS QUILT, AND THE RESULT IS *BIG LOVE*. JUST AS WITH *BIG BLOOMS* (PAGE 15), *BIG LOVE* APPEARS TO BE MADE OF ANGULAR SHAPES, BUT IT IS SIMPLY MADE OF SQUARES THAT ARE SEWN TOGETHER DIAGONALLY.

Fabrics

The X's and O's in the *Big Love* quilt top are made from two different colors — one light and one dark of each. Solids and prints are both fine to use for the X's and O's; if you use prints, keep them small in scale and don't use directional prints. Make sure there is strong contrast with the background fabric, so that the hugs and kisses pop.

The quilt back is made of an "X" and "O" feature section that is constructed the same way as the quilt top. Fabric panels are added to this feature to finish off the back. Large-scale prints will work just fine for these panels.

The pictured *Big Love* is made in the Bahamas palette using aqua and yellow solids for the X's and O's and a white-on-white print for the background. Make a quilt like mine, or choose your palette for *Big Love* from the Palette Suggestions (page 48).

Big Love lap-size quilt back

MATERIALS

Yardages are based on 40˝-wide fabric.

Material	Description	Lap quilt (45˝ × 60˝)	Twin quilt (60˝ × 90˝)
Fabric 1	Dark yellow solid for the dark X's	1 yard	2 yards
Fabric 2	Light yellow solid for the light X's	1 yard	1¼ yards
Fabric 3	Dark aqua solid for the dark O's	1 yard	1¼ yards
Fabric 4	Light aqua solid for the light O's	1 yard	2 yards
Fabric 5	Off-white print for the backgrounds	1½ yards	2½ yards
Fabric 6	Multicolored print for the back panels	2 yards	4¼ yards*
Fabric 7	Light yellow solid for the binding	½ yard	¾ yard
Batting		53˝ × 68˝	68˝ × 98˝

* The narrower back panel requires piecing. To avoid piecing, you'll need 5⅝ yards.

CUTTING

Refer to Staying Organized (page 5) for tips on keeping track of your cut fabric.

When subcutting strips, cut the longest pieces first.

Material	Lap quilt (45″ × 60″)	Twin quilt (60″ × 90″)
Fabric 1	Cut 4 strips 8″ × width of fabric; subcut into: 16 squares 8″ × 8″ (1a)	Cut 8 strips 8″ × width of fabric; subcut into: 34 squares 8″ × 8″ (1a) 2 rectangles 8″ × 11¾″ (1b)
Fabric 2	Cut 4 strips 8″ × width of fabric; subcut into: 14 squares 8″ × 8″ (2a) 2 rectangles 8″ × 11¾″ (2b)	Cut 5 strips 8″ × width of fabric; subcut into: 24 squares 8″ × 8″ (2a)
Fabric 3	Cut 4 strips 8″ × width of fabric; subcut into: 14 squares 8″ × 8″ (3a) 2 rectangles 8″ × 11¾″ (3b)	Cut 5 strips 8″ × width of fabric; subcut into: 24 squares 8″ × 8″ (3a)
Fabric 4	Cut 4 strips 8″ × width of fabric; subcut into: 16 squares 8″ × 8″ (4a)	Cut 8 strips 8″ × width of fabric; subcut into: 34 squares 8″ × 8″ (4a) 2 rectangles 8″ × 11¾″ (4b)
Fabric 5	Cut 11 strips 3½″ × width of fabric; subcut into: 121 squares 3½″ × 3½″ (5c) Cut 1 strip 7¼″ × width of fabric; subcut into: 3 squares 3½″ × 3½″ (5c) 4 squares 7¼″ × 7¼″ (5d)	Cut 21 strips 3½″ × width of fabric; subcut into: 231 squares 3½″ × 3½″ (5c) Cut 1 strip 7¼″ × width of fabric; subcut into: 5 squares 3½″ × 3½″ (5c) 4 squares 7¼″ × 7¼″ (5d)
Fabric 6	Cut 1 piece 26¾″ × 68″ (7e) Cut 1 piece 11¾″ × 68″ (7f)	Cut 1 piece 34¼″ × 98″ (6g) Cut 2 pieces 19¼″ × 49¼″ (6h)*
Fabric 7	Cut 6 strips 2½″ × width of fabric for binding	Cut 9 strips 2½″ × width of fabric for binding

* Carefully cut the fabric so that the print will match when the pieces are joined. OR if you have 5⅝ yards, cut 1 piece 19¼″ × 98″ (6h).

Preparation

On the wrong side of each background square, draw a diagonal stitching line from one corner to the opposite corner.

- -

Drawing Stitching Lines

Use either a light pencil line or a disappearing ink marker when drawing stitching lines on fabric. It also helps to place fabric on a sandpaper board that will hold the fabric in place while you draw. See Resources (page 111).

- -

Construction

Big Love is assembled in quarter-blocks or quadrants that are further assembled into rows that form the quilt top. For the quilt back, the quadrants are assembled into columns. All seam allowances are ¼″ and are pressed to one side. To create nesting seams, press the seams toward the background in half the quadrants for each fabric and press toward the X or O fabric in the other half. When sewing quadrants together, for odd-numbered rows or columns, press the seams in one direction; for even-numbered rows or columns, press the seams in the opposite direction. Between rows or columns, press all the seams in one direction.

QUADRANTS

1. With right sides together, pin the background pieces onto the X and O pieces as shown.

Pinning Squares

When pinning squares that are to be sewn on the diagonal, use at least two pins. Insert one pin perpendicular to the sewing line and the other parallel to the sewing line, leaving sufficient space for the presser foot to pass by. This will prevent the square from slipping out of position when sewing.

Salvaging Scraps

If you like working with scraps, save the trimmings for another project. There will be enough to make a throw pillow or small quilt.

2. Sew along the marked diagonal lines. Trim off corners ¼″ away from the sewing lines, and press. For each fabric, press the seams toward the background in half of the quadrants and toward fabric 1 through 4 in the other half. For Quadrants E through L, wait until you've arranged the quadrants into columns for the quilt back before pressing.

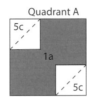

Quadrant A

Lap size: Make 16.
Twin size: Make 34.

Quadrant B

Lap size: Make 14.
Twin size: Make 24.

Quadrant C

Lap size: Make 14.
Twin size: Make 24.

Quadrant D

Lap size: Make 16.
Twin size: Make 34.

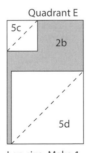

Quadrant E

Lap size: Make 1.

Quadrant F

Twin size: Make 1.

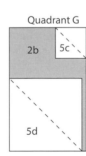

Quadrant G

Lap size: Make 1.

Quadrant H

Twin size: Make 1.

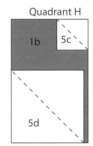

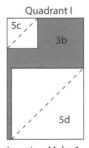

Quadrant I

Lap size: Make 1.

Quadrant J

Twin size: Make 1.

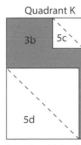

Quadrant K

Lap size: Make 1.

Quadrant L

Twin size: Make 1.

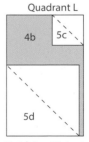

QUILT TOP

Refer to either the lap-size quilt assembly diagram or the twin-size quilt assembly diagram.

1. Arrange the quadrants in rows, rotating them as needed. Sew together the quadrants in pairs.

2. Sew together the pairs to assemble the rows and press.

3. Sew together the rows to assemble the quilt top and press.

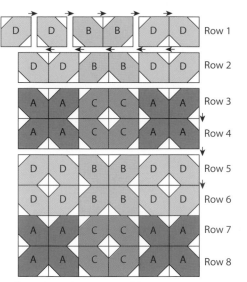

Lap-size quilt top assembly

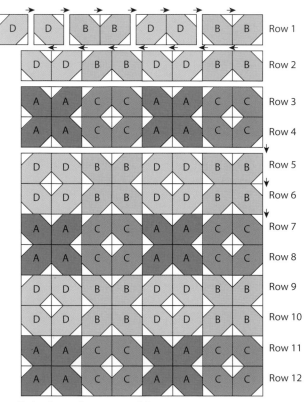

Twin-size quilt top assembly

QUILT BACK

Refer to either the lap-size quilt back assembly diagram or the twin-size quilt back assembly diagram.

1. Sew together the quadrants into pairs and press. Note: If you are piecing the back panel for the twin-size quilt, match the print pattern of the 6h pieces.

2. Sew together the pairs into columns and press.

3. Sew together the columns to assemble the quilt back and press.

FINISHING

Refer to Quilt Finishing (page 103) for instructions on sandwiching, basting, quilting, and binding.

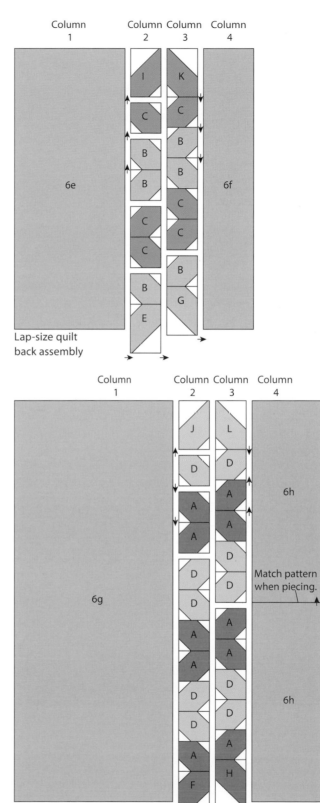

Lap-size quilt back assembly

Twin-size quilt back assembly

Palette Suggestions

Express your affection with a *Big Love* quilt in the Valentine palette. If you're looking for something masculine, try the Metallic palette. Some neutral paint, dark gray sheets, and a few linen throw pillows are all that is needed to turn a plain bedroom into a sophisticated retreat.

XOXOXO!

Valentine

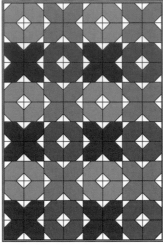

Metallic

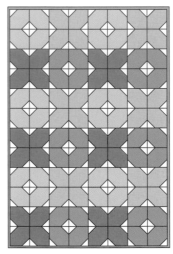

Bahamas

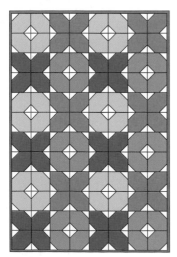

Citrus

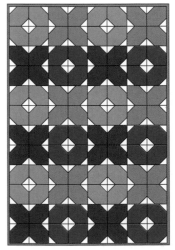

Boyfriend

Violets

Big Pennant

Big Pennant lap-size quilt—Circus palette, made by Barbara Cain

Finished quilts:
45″ × 60″ lap size
60″ × 90″ twin size

THE PENNANTS THAT MAKE THIS FESTIVE QUILT ARE JUST SIMPLE, ELONGATED ISOSCELES TRIANGLES. THEY ARE SIZABLE—15″ WIDE AND 30″ LONG WHEN FINISHED—AND ARE BY FAR THE LARGEST COMPONENT OF ALL THE QUILTS IN THIS BOOK. THAT MAKES *BIG PENNANT* SUPER FAST TO PUT TOGETHER. IF YOU'RE TIGHT ON TIME, YOU MIGHT WANT TO TRY THIS ONE.

Fabrics

Big Pennant is made with three colorful fabrics and one neutral background fabric. Solids and prints work just fine for this quilt; however, when using prints, be sure to use either nondirectional or two-way directional designs.

The quilt back is made of a pennant feature section that is constructed in the same way as the quilt top. Fabric panels are situated on both sides of this feature and complete the back.

The pictured *Big Pennant* uses the Circus palette. This vivid scheme is quite playful and will certainly bring a cheerful atmosphere to any space. For more color ideas, refer to Palette Suggestions (page 57).

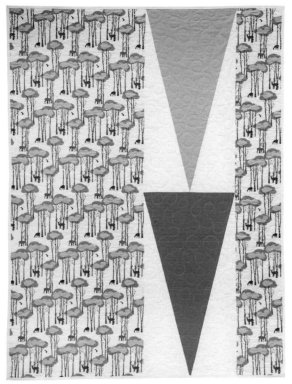

Big Pennant lap-size quilt back

MATERIALS

Yardages are based on 40″-wide fabric.

Material	Description	Lap quilt (45″ × 60″)	Twin quilt (60″ × 90″)
Fabric 1	Chartreuse solid for the pennants	1 yard	1½ yards
Fabric 2	Jade solid for the pennants	⅞ yard	1½ yards
Fabric 3	Orange solid for the pennants	1 yard	1½ yards
Fabric 4	White print for the background	2¼ yards	3⅝ yards
Fabric 5	Multicolored print for the back panels	2 yards	4¼ yards*
Fabric 6	White solid for the binding	½ yard	¾ yard
Batting		53″ × 68″	68″ × 98″
Template material	Mat board, poster board, or heavy cardboard	36″ × 36″	36″ × 36″

* The narrower back panel requires piecing. To avoid piecing, you'll need 5⅝ yards.

CUTTING

Refer to Staying Organized (page 5) for tips on keeping track of your cut fabric. Cut all of the triangles on the crosswise grain of the fabric. Refer to Cutting Diagrams for Selected Quilts (page 87).

Important! Starch your fabric before cutting triangles. Refer to Working with Bias Edges (page 6).

Material	Lap quilt (45˝ × 60˝)	Twin quilt (60˝ × 90˝)
Fabric 1	Cut 2 a triangles (1a) Cut 1 f extended triangle (1f)	Cut 4 a triangles (1a) Cut 1 f extended triangle (1f)
Fabric 2	Cut 2 a triangles (2a)	Cut 5 a triangles (2a)
Fabric 3	Cut 3 a triangles (3a)	Cut 5 a triangles (3a)
Fabric 4	Cut 4 a triangles (4a) Cut 3 b edge triangles (4b) Cut 3 c edge triangles (4c) Cut 1 d extended edge triangle (4d) Cut 1 e extended edge triangle (4e)	Cut 9 a triangles (4a) Cut 5 b edge triangles (4b) Cut 5 c edge triangles (4c) Cut 1 d extended edge triangle (4d) Cut 1 e extended edge triangle (4e)
Fabric 5	Cut 1 piece 26¾˝ × 68˝ (5g) Cut 1 piece 11¾˝ × 68˝ (5h)	Cut 1 piece 34¼˝ × 98˝ (5i) Cut 2 pieces 19¼˝ × 49¼˝ (5j)*
Fabric 6	Cut 6 strips 2½˝ × width of fabric for binding	Cut 9 strips 2½˝ × width of fabric for binding

* Carefully cut the fabric so that the print will match when the pieces are joined. OR if you have 5⅝ yards, cut 1 piece 19¼˝ × 98˝ (5j).

Make Templates

Refer to Making and Using Templates (page 6).

Make templates for the a triangle, the b/c edge triangle, the d/e extended edge triangle, and the f extended triangle, as shown.

- -

Piecing Template Boards

If you don't have access to mat board or poster board large enough for these templates, use two smaller boards and tape them together.

- -

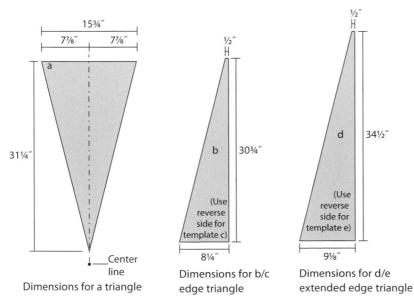

Dimensions for a triangle

Dimensions for b/c edge triangle

Dimensions for d/e extended edge triangle

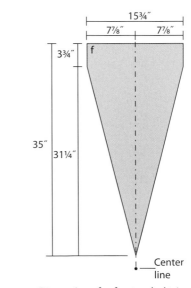

Dimensions for f extended triangle

Construction

Big Pennant is assembled in triangular pairs that are further assembled into rows that form the quilt top. For the quilt back, the pairs are assembled into blocks and then into a column. All seam allowances are ¼″ and are pressed to one side. When sewing the triangle pairs, press the seams toward the pennant fabric; when joining the pairs into rows, press the seams toward the background. Between rows and columns, press all the seams in one direction.

TRIANGLE PAIRS

To ensure proper alignment of triangle pairs, carefully refer to the assembly diagrams that follow.

Triangle to Triangle

1. With right sides up, place the triangles to be paired side by side. Flip one triangle onto the other along the edge to be sewn.

2. Keeping the edges to be sewn aligned, slightly shift the pieces so that the lower pennant triangle extends beyond the upper, until the lower triangle, the upper triangle, and the ¼″ seamline all intersect at the same point. Gently pin and sew together the pieces using a ¼″ seam. Press seams toward the pennant fabric.

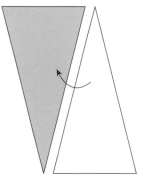

Pair triangles side by side.

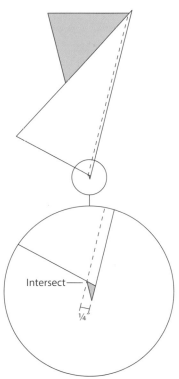

Align, shift, and sew.

Edge Triangle to Triangle

In a manner similar to Triangle to Triangle (page 53), sew together the pieces as shown.

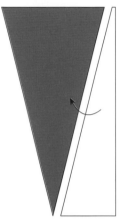

1. Pair triangles side by side.

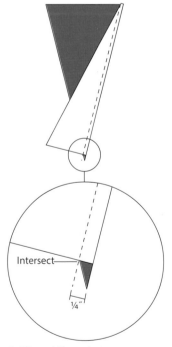

2. Align, shift, and sew.

Extended Edge Triangle to Triangle

1. With right sides up, place pennant triangle a and extended edge triangle 4d side by side. Flip 4d onto the a triangle along the edge to be sewn.

Pair triangles side by side.

2. Keeping the edges to be sewn aligned, slightly shift the pieces so that a extends beyond 4d, until a, 4d, and the ¼″ seamline all intersect at the same point. Gently pin and sew the ¼″ seam.

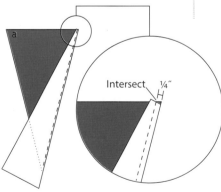

Align, shift, and sew.

3. Flip 4d to its face-up position and press the seam allowance toward the pennant fabric. Trim off the protruding portion of 4d.

Trim.

4. Repeat Steps 1 and 2 to add piece 4e to the 3a/4d or 2a/4d assembly. Flip 4e to its face-up position and press toward the background.

Add piece 4e.

QUILT TOP

Refer to either the lap-size quilt assembly diagram or the twin-size quilt assembly diagram.

1. Sew together the pairs into rows and press toward the background.

2. If any stretching has occurred, trim the edge triangles as needed to align with the center triangles; the pennant rows should measure 30½˝ high. This consists of 30¼˝ from the center of the pennant base to its opposite point, plus a ¼˝ seam allowance above the point. Trim any dog-ear triangles that extend into the seam allowances.

3. Sew together the rows to assemble the quilt top and press.

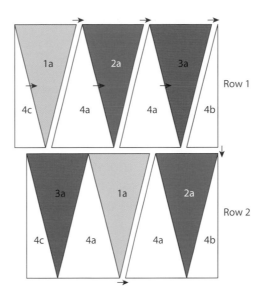

Lap-size quilt top assembly

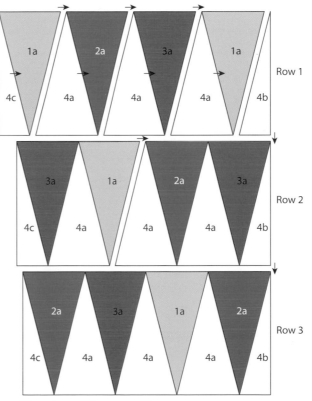

Twin-size quilt top assembly

QUILT BACK

Refer to either the lap-size quilt back assembly diagram or the twin-size quilt back assembly diagram.

1. Sew together the triangles into blocks and press. Note: If you are piecing the back panel for the twin-size quilt, match the print pattern of the 5j pieces.

2. Sew together the blocks into a column and press.

3. Sew together the columns to assemble the quilt back and press.

FINISHING

Refer to Quilt Finishing (page 103) for instructions on sandwiching, basting, quilting, and binding.

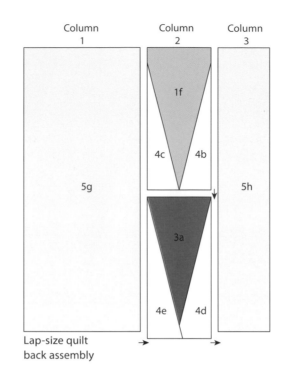

Lap-size quilt back assembly

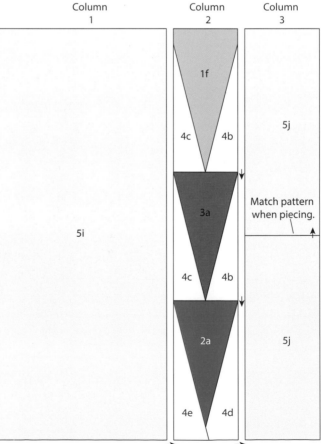

Twin-size quilt back assembly

Palette Suggestions

These palettes illustrate just a few ways in which *Big Pennant* can transform through the use of color. Choose one of these or create your own that echoes your personality.

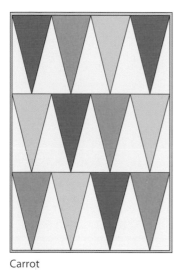

Carrot

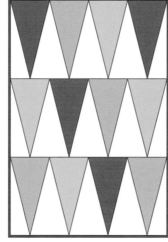

Hollyhock

Peppermint

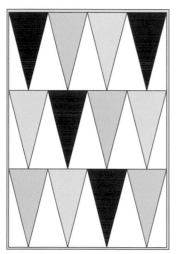

Vineyard

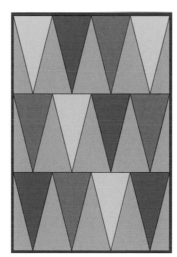

Black Ice

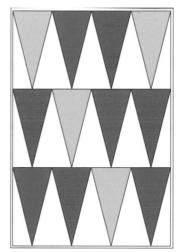

Circus

Big Plaid

Big Plaid lap-size quilt—Dad palette, made by Barbara Cain

Finished quilts:

45″ × 60″ lap size

60″ × 90″ twin size

WHO DOESN'T LOVE A PLAID? THIS STYLISH PLAID PATTERN IS THE SIMPLEST OF DESIGNS; IT IS MADE FROM NOTHING MORE THAN STRAIGHTFORWARD RECTANGLES. SHOW OFF YOUR SMART STYLE AND WHIP UP AN EASY, BIG PLAID QUILT!

Fabrics

Big Plaid is made with two main colors; one light and one dark value of each. To maintain the value play that makes this plaid pattern pop, use of solids or small-scale prints works best.

The quilt back is made of a plaid feature section that is constructed the same way as the quilt top. Fabric panels line each side of the feature and finish off the back.

This *Big Plaid* is made from solid fabrics in the Dad palette. The brown and yellow hues remind me of a casual plaid shirt that my father often wore. Get inspired by the Palette Suggestions (page 64) or choose your two favorite colors (one light and one dark of each) and build your own personal plaid.

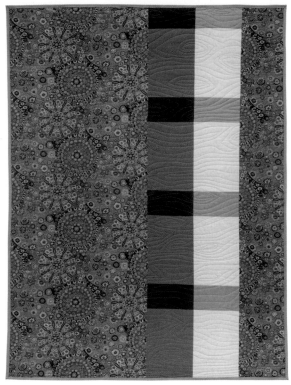

Big Plaid lap-size quilt back

MATERIALS

Yardages are based on 40″-wide fabric.

Material	Description	Lap quilt (45″ × 60″)	Twin quilt (60″ × 90″)
Fabric 1	Dark brown solid for the plaid	¾ yard	1⅛ yards
Fabric 2	Light brown solid for the plaid	1½ yards	2⅛ yards
Fabric 3	Dark gold solid for the plaid	¾ yard	1⅛ yards
Fabric 4	Light gold solid for the plaid	1½ yards	2⅛ yards
Fabric 5	Multicolored print for the back panels	2 yards	4¼ yards*
Fabric 6	Dark gold solid for the binding	½ yard	¾ yard
Batting		53″ × 68″	68″ × 98″

* The narrower back panel requires piecing. To avoid piecing, you'll need 5⅝ yards.

CUTTING

Refer to Staying Organized (page 5) for tips on keeping track of your cut fabric.

When subcutting strips, cut the longest pieces first.

Material	Lap quilt (45″ × 60″)	Twin quilt (60″ × 90″)

Fabric 1	Cut 3 strips 4½″ × width of fabric; subcut into:
	  15 rectangles 4½″ × 8″ (1a)
	Cut 1 strip 8¼″ × width of fabric; subcut into:
	  1 rectangle 8¼″ × 8″ (1c)
		Cut 6 strips 4½″ × width of fabric; subcut into:
		  29 rectangles 4½″ × 8″ (1a)
		Cut 1 strip 8¼″ × width of fabric; subcut into:
		  1 rectangle 8¼″ × 8″ (1c)

Fabric 2	Cut 3 strips 11½″ × width of fabric; subcut into:
	  15 rectangles 11½″ × 8″ (2b)
	Cut 1 strip 15¼″ × width of fabric; subcut into:
	  1 rectangle 15¼″ × 8″ (2d)
		Cut 5 strips 11½″ × width of fabric; subcut into:
		  25 rectangles 11½″ × 8″ (2b)
		Cut 1 strip 15¼″ × width of fabric; subcut into:
		  4 rectangles 8″ × 11½″ (2b)
		  1 rectangle 15¼″ × 8″ (2d)

Fabric 3	Cut 3 strips 4½″ × width of fabric; subcut into:
	  15 rectangles 4½″ × 8″ (3a)
	Cut 1 strip 8¼″ × width of fabric; subcut into:
	  1 rectangle 8¼″ × 8″ (3c)
		Cut 6 strips 4½″ × width of fabric; subcut into:
		  29 rectangles 4½″ × 8″ (3a)
		Cut 1 strip 8¼″ × width of fabric; subcut into:
		  1 rectangle 8¼″ × 8″ (3c)

Fabric 4	Cut 3 strips 11½″ × width of fabric; subcut into:
	  15 rectangles 11½″ × 8″ (4b)
	Cut 1 strip 15¼″ × width of fabric; subcut into:
	  1 rectangle 15¼″ × 8″ (4d)
		Cut 5 strips 11½″ × width of fabric; subcut into:
		  25 rectangles 11½″ × 8″ (4b)
		Cut 1 strip 15¼″ × width of fabric; subcut into:
		  4 rectangles 8″ × 11½″ (4b)
		  1 rectangle 15¼″ × 8″ (4d)

Fabric 5	Cut 1 piece 26¾″ × 68″ (5e) Cut 1 piece 11¾″ × 68″ (5f)	Cut 1 piece 34¼″ × 98″ (5g) Cut 2 pieces 19¼″ × 49¼″ (5h)*
Fabric 6	Cut 6 strips 2½″ × width of fabric for binding	Cut 9 strips 2½″ × width of fabric for binding

* Carefully cut the fabric so that the print will match when the pieces are joined. OR if you have 5⅝ yards, cut 1 piece 19¼″ × 98″ (5h).

Construction

Big Plaid is assembled in columns. All seam allowances are ¼″ and are pressed to one side. For odd-numbered columns, press the seams in one direction; for even-numbered columns, press the seams in the opposite direction. Between columns, press all the seams in one direction.

QUILT TOP

Refer to either the lap-size quilt assembly diagram or the twin-size quilt assembly diagram.

1. Sew together the pieces into pairs and press.

2. Sew together the pairs into columns and press.

3. Sew together the columns to assemble the quilt top and press.

Lap-size quilt top assembly

Twin-size quilt top assembly

QUILT BACK

Refer to either the lap-size quilt back assembly diagram or the twin-size quilt back assembly diagram.

1. Sew together the pieces into pairs and press. Note: If you are piecing the back panel for the twin-size quilt, match the print pattern of the 5h pieces.

2. Sew together the pairs into columns and press.

3. Sew together the columns to assemble the quilt back and press.

FINISHING

Refer to Quilt Finishing (page 103) for instructions on sandwiching, basting, quilting, and binding.

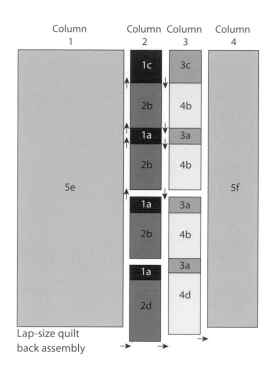

Lap-size quilt back assembly

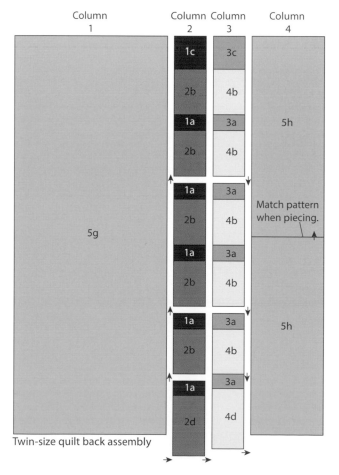

Twin-size quilt back assembly

Palette Suggestions

Big Plaid can be made to represent any of your favorite things. Simply create a two-color palette that signifies your theme, like school colors, sports team uniforms, bridal party dresses—the possibilities are endless. You could also choose from one of these alternate suggestions.

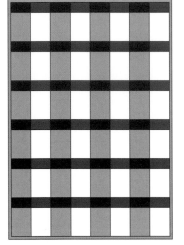

Sugar Plum

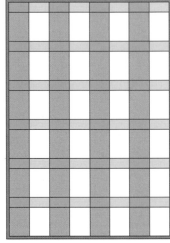

Industrial

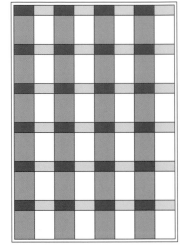

Saint Patrick

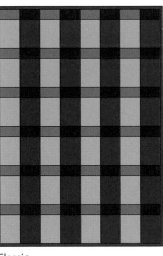

Surf and Turf

Classic

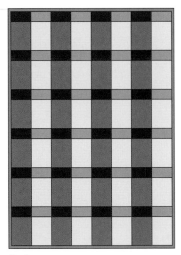

Dad

Big Plus

Big Plus twin-size quilt—Race Car palette, made by Barbara Cain

Finished quilts:
45˝ × 60˝ lap size
60˝ × 90˝ twin size

THE PLUS SYMBOL HAS MANY MEANINGS: "MORE," "POSITIVE," ADD," JUST TO NAME A FEW. MAKING A *BIG PLUS* QUILT WILL CERTAINLY BE A POSITIVE EXPERIENCE, AS YOU WILL BE PLEASED AT HOW QUICKLY THIS HIGH-IMPACT, EASY QUILT COMES TOGETHER.

Fabrics

Big Plus is made with six colorful fabrics. Solids and directional prints can both be used, but try to keep the scale of the prints on the small side. Bold, busy prints will detract from the shape of the plusses, and you really want these to be visible.

The quilt back is made with fabric panels and a plus feature section that is constructed the same way as the quilt top. The back panels can easily handle a larger scale print, as they are quite sizable.

The pictured *Big Plus* is made from both solid and print fabrics in the Race Car palette. The brilliant red and yellow plusses really stand out and are reminiscent of the vibrant paint schemes of race cars.

Big Plus twin-size quilt back

MATERIALS

Yardages are based on 40″-wide fabric.

Material	Description	Lap quilt (45″ × 60″)	Twin quilt (60″ × 90″)
Fabric 1	White print for the plusses	¾ yard	1¼ yards
Fabric 2	Black print for the plusses	¾ yard	1¼ yards
Fabric 3	Light gray solid for the plusses	¾ yard	1¼ yards
Fabric 4	Dark gray solid for the plusses	¾ yard	1¼ yards
Fabric 5	Bright yellow solid for the plusses	1⅛ yards	1¼ yards
Fabric 6	Bright red solid for the plusses	1⅛ yards	1¼ yards
Fabric 7	Black-and-white print for the back panels	2 yards	4¼ yards*
Fabric 8	Black solid for the binding	½ yard	¾ yard
Batting		53″ × 68″	68″ × 98″

* The narrower back panel requires piecing. To avoid piecing, you'll need 5⅝ yards.

CUTTING

Refer to Staying Organized (page 5) for tips on keeping track of your cut fabric.

When subcutting strips, cut the longest pieces first.

Material	Lap quilt (45″ × 60″)	Twin quilt (60″ × 90″)
Fabric 1	Cut 1 strip 23″ × width of fabric; subcut into: 　4 squares 8″ × 8″ (1a) 　2 rectangles 8″ × 23″ (1c)	Cut 2 strips 8″ × width of fabric; subcut into: 　7 squares 8″ × 8″ (1a) Cut 1 strip 23″ × width of fabric; subcut into: 　4 rectangles 8″ × 23″ (1c) 　1 rectangle 8″ × 11¾″ (1d)
Fabric 2	Cut 1 strip 23″ × width of fabric; subcut into: 　4 squares 8″ × 8″ (2a) 　1 rectangle 8″ × 15½″ (2b) 　1 rectangle 8″ × 23″ (2c)	Cut 2 strips 8″ × width of fabric; subcut into: 　7 squares 8″ × 8″ (2a) Cut 1 strip 23″ × width of fabric; subcut into: 　1 rectangle 8″ × 15½″ (2b) 　4 rectangles 8″ × 23″ (2c)
Fabric 3	Cut 1 strip 23″ × width of fabric; subcut into: 　4 squares 8″ × 8″ (3a) 　2 rectangles 8″ × 23″ (3c)	Cut 2 strips 8″ × width of fabric; subcut into: 　10 squares 8″ × 8″ (3a) Cut 1 strip 23″ × width of fabric; subcut into: 　1 rectangle 8″ × 15½″ (3b) 　2 rectangles 8″ × 23″ (3c) 　1 rectangle 8″ × 11¾″ (3d)
Fabric 4	Cut 1 strip 23″ × width of fabric; subcut into: 　4 squares 8″ × 8″ (4a) 　1 rectangle 8″ × 23″ (4c) 　1 rectangle 8″ × 11¾″ (4d)	Cut 2 strips 8″ × width of fabric; subcut into: 　10 squares 8″ × 8″ (3a) Cut 1 strip 23″ × width of fabric; subcut into: 　1 rectangle 8″ × 15½″ (3b) 　2 rectangles 8″ × 23″ (3c) 　1 rectangle 8″ × 11¾″ (3d)
Fabric 5	Cut 1 strip 8″ × width of fabric; subcut into: 　5 squares 8″ × 8″ (5a) Cut 1 strip 26¾″ × width of fabric; subcut into: 　1 rectangle 8″ × 15½″ (5b) 　1 rectangle 8″ × 23″ (5c) 　1 rectangle 8″ × 26¾″ (5e)	Cut 2 strips 8″ × width of fabric; subcut into: 　7 squares 8″ × 8″ (5a) Cut 1 strip 23″ × width of fabric; subcut into: 　4 rectangles 8″ × 23″ (5c) 　1 rectangle 8″ × 11¾″ (5d)
Fabric 6	Cut 1 strip 8″ × width of fabric; subcut into: 　5 squares 8″ × 8″ (6a) Cut 1 strip 26¾″ × width of fabric; subcut into: 　1 rectangle 8″ × 15½″ (6b) 　1 rectangle 8″ × 23″ (6c) 　1 rectangle 8″ × 11¾″ (6d) 　1 rectangle 8″ × 26¾″ (6e)	Cut 2 strips 8″ × width of fabric; subcut into: 　7 squares 8″ × 8″ (6a) Cut 1 strip 23″ × width of fabric; subcut into: 　1 rectangle 8″ × 15½″ (6b) 　4 rectangles 8″ × 23″ (6c)
Fabric 7	Cut 1 piece 26¾″ × 68″ (7f) Cut 1 piece 11¾″ × 68″ (7g)	Cut 1 piece 34¼″ × 98″ (7h) Cut 2 pieces 19¼″ × 49¼″ (7i)*
Fabric 8	Cut 6 strips 2½″ × width of fabric for binding	Cut 9 strips 2½″ × width of fabric for binding

* Carefully cut the fabric so that the print will match when the pieces are joined. OR if you have 5⅝ yards, cut 1 piece 19¼″ × 98″ (7i).

Construction

Big Plus is assembled in columns. All seam allowances are ¼˝ and are pressed to one side. For odd-numbered columns, press the seams in one direction; for even-numbered columns, press the seams in the opposite direction. Between columns, press all the seams in one direction.

QUILT TOP

Refer to either the lap-size quilt assembly diagram or the twin-size quilt assembly diagram.

1. Sew together the pieces into pairs and press.

2. Sew together the pairs into columns and press.

3. Sew together the columns to assemble the quilt top and press.

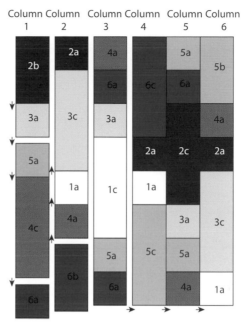

Lap-size quilt top assembly

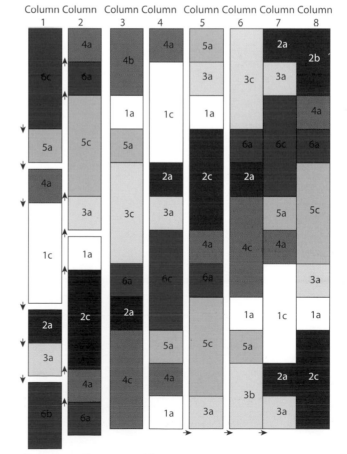

Twin-size quilt top assembly

QUILT BACK

Refer to either the lap-size quilt back assembly diagram or the twin-size quilt back assembly diagram.

1. Sew together the pieces into pairs and press. Note: If you are piecing the back panel for the twin-size quilt, match the print pattern of the 7i pieces.

2. Sew together the pairs into columns and press.

3. Sew together the columns to assemble the quilt back and press.

FINISHING

Refer to Quilt Finishing (page 103) for instructions on sandwiching, basting, quilting, and binding.

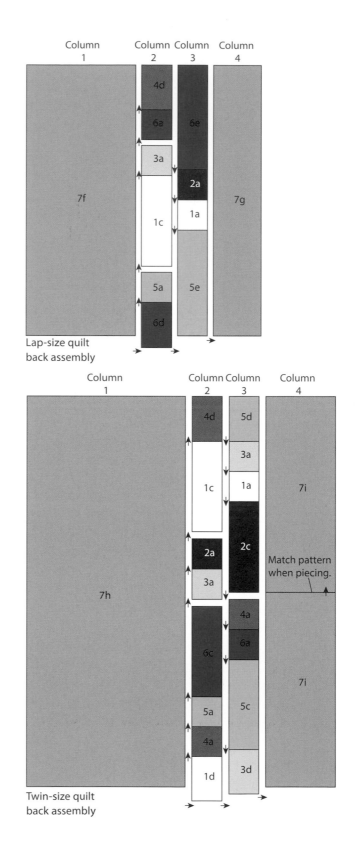

Palette Suggestions

These are just a sampling of what can be done with the *Big Plus* pattern. Looking for something to brighten your guest room? How about the Fresh Cherries palette? This quilt and a few bright green accents can turn a neutral space into an inviting, casual environment. For a little more drama, consider the Koi Pond palette. Lots of white with deep blue and orange accents would make a great 70's retro look. Add a shag rug and you're done.

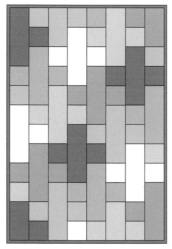

Caribbean

Girly

Race Car

Tutti-frutti

Koi Pond

Fresh Cherries

Big Sawtooth

Big Sawtooth lap-size quilt—Cosmos palette, made by Barbara Cain

Finished quilts:

45″ × 60″ lap size

60″ × 90″ twin size

BIG SAWTOOTH IS ONE OF THREE QUILT PATTERNS IN THIS BOOK MADE WITH ISOSCELES TRIANGLES. FOR THIS QUILT, THE TRIANGLES POINT BOTH LEFT AND RIGHT AND ARE SEPARATED BY SASHING STRIPS. THIS ARRANGEMENT GIVES THE QUILT A MOCK CHEVRON LOOK.

Fabrics

Big Sawtooth is made with two colorful triangle fabrics, one background fabric, and one sashing fabric. Solids and prints are both good to use, but to save on yardage, only nondirectional or two-way directional prints should be chosen for the triangles.

The quilt back is made of a sawtooth feature section that is constructed the same way as the quilt top. Fabric panels are also used on the back; large-scale prints work well for these.

This *Big Sawtooth* quilt is made from solid and print fabrics in the Cosmos palette. For other color ideas, refer to Palette Suggestions (page 79).

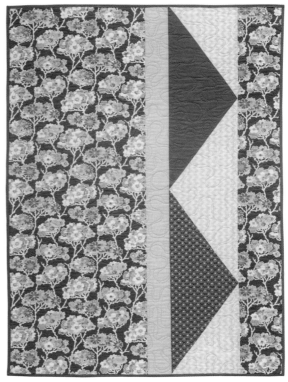

Big Sawtooth lap-size quilt back

MATERIALS

Yardages are based on 40″-wide fabric.

Material	Description	Lap quilt (45″ × 60″)	Twin quilt (60″ × 90″)
Fabric 1	Gray solid for the sawtooth triangles	1½ yards	2 yards
Fabric 2	Magenta print for the sawtooth triangles	1 yard	2 yards
Fabric 3	Off-white print for the background triangles	1¾ yards	2¾ yards
Fabric 4	Bright green print for the strips	1⅛ yards	2⅛ yards
Fabric 5	Multicolored print for the back panels	2 yards	4¼ yards*
Fabric 6	Gray solid for the binding	½ yard	¾ yard
Batting		53″ × 68″	68″ × 98″
Template material	Mat board, poster board, or heavy cardboard	30″ × 36″	30″ × 36″

* The narrower back panel requires piecing. To avoid piecing, you'll need 5⅝ yards.

CUTTING

Refer to Staying Organized (page 5) for tips on keeping track of your cut fabric.

Refer to Cutting Diagrams for Selected Quilts (page 87).

Important! Starch your fabric before cutting triangles. Refer to Working with Bias Edges (page 6).

Material	Lap quilt (45″ × 60″)	Twin quilt (60″ × 90″)
Fabric 1	Cut 5 a triangles (1a)	Cut 8 a triangles (1a)
Fabric 2	Cut 3 a triangles (2a)	Cut 7 a triangles (2a)
Fabric 3	Cut 4 a triangles (3a) Cut 3 b edge triangles (3b) Cut 3 c edge triangles (3c) Cut 1 d extended edge triangle (3d) Cut 1 e extended edge triangle (3e)	Cut 10 a triangles (3a) Cut 4 b edge triangles (3b) Cut 4 c edge triangles (3c) Cut 1 d extended edge triangle (3d) Cut 1 e extended edge triangle (3e)
Fabric 4*	Cut 6 strips 4½″ × 30½″ (4f) Cut 2 strips 4½″ × 34¼″ (4g)	Cut 13 strips 4½″ × 30½″ (4f) Cut 2 strips 4½″ × 34¼″ (4g)
Fabric 5	Cut 1 piece 26¾″ × 68″ (5h) Cut 1 piece 11¾″ × 68″ (5i)	Cut 1 piece 34¼″ × 98″ (5j) Cut 2 pieces 19¼″ × 49¼″ (5k)**
Fabric 6	Cut 6 strips 2½″ × width of fabric for the binding	Cut 9 strips 2½″ × width of fabric for the binding

* Cut all strips from Fabric 4 on the lengthwise grain (parallel to the selvages).

** Carefully cut the fabric so that the print will match when the pieces are joined. OR if you have 5⅝ yards, cut 1 piece 19¼″ × 98″ (5k).

Make Templates

Refer to Making and Using Templates (page 6).

Make templates for the a triangle, b/c edge triangle, and d/e extended edge triangles, as shown.

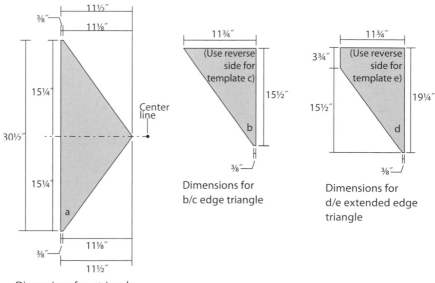

Dimensions for a triangle

Dimensions for b/c edge triangle

Dimensions for d/e extended edge triangle

Construction

Big Sawtooth is assembled in triangular pairs that are further assembled into columns that form the quilt top and back. All seam allowances are ¼″ and are pressed to one side. For odd-numbered columns, press the seams in one direction; for even-numbered columns, press the seams in the opposite direction. Work with one column at a time when sewing triangles together in pairs. Between columns, press all the seams in one direction.

TRIANGLE PAIRS

To ensure proper alignment of triangle pairs, carefully refer to the assembly diagrams that follow.

Triangle to Triangle

1. With right sides up, place the triangles to be paired side by side. Flip one triangle onto the other along the edge to be sewn.

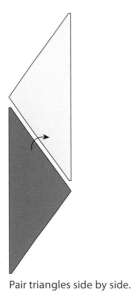

Pair triangles side by side.

2. The diagonal edges of the triangles are exactly the same size. Align these accurately, matching the outermost points of both triangles. Gently pin together the triangles and sew ¼″ away from the aligned edge. Flip the upper triangle to its face-up position and press the seam allowance in the desired direction.

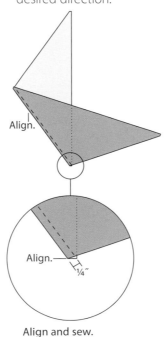

Align.

Align. ¼″

Align and sew.

Triangle to Edge Triangle

1. With right sides up, place the triangles to be paired side by side. Flip the larger triangle onto the smaller background triangle along the edge to be sewn.

Pair triangles side by side.

2. Align the edges to be sewn and slightly shift the pieces so that the lower edge triangle, the upper triangle, and the ¼″ seamline all intersect at the same point. Gently pin the triangles together and sew ¼″ away from the aligned edges. Flip the upper triangle to its face-up position and press the seam allowance in the desired direction.

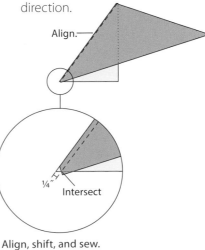

Align.

¼″ Intersect

Align, shift, and sew.

QUILT TOP

Refer to either the lap-size quilt assembly diagram or the twin-size quilt assembly diagram.

1. Sew together the pairs to assemble columns and press. If stretching has occurred, trim the sawtooth columns to a width of 11½″. This consists of 11¼″ from the center of the triangle base to its opposite point, plus a ¼″ seam allowance from the point to the edge of the column.

2. Sew together the columns to assemble the quilt top and press.

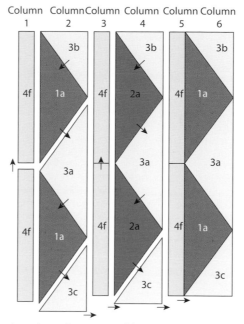

Lap-size quilt top assembly

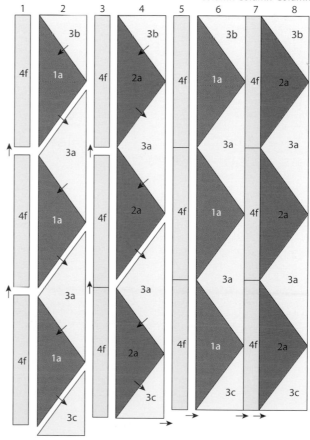

Twin-size quilt top assembly

QUILT BACK

Refer to either the lap-size quilt back assembly diagram or the twin-size quilt back assembly diagram.

1. Sew together the pieces into pairs and press. Note: If you are piecing the back panel for the twin-size quilt, match the print pattern of the 5k pieces.

2. Sew together the pairs into columns and press.

3. Sew together the columns to assemble the quilt back and press.

FINISHING

Refer to Quilt Finishing (page 103) for instructions on sandwiching, basting, quilting, and binding.

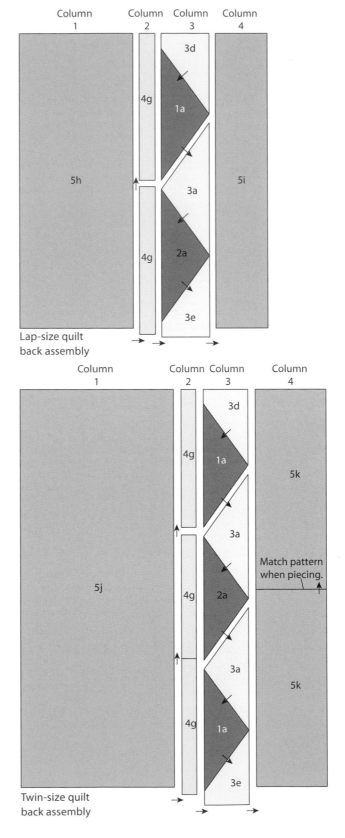

Lap-size quilt back assembly

Twin-size quilt back assembly

Palette Suggestions

The *Big Sawtooth* quilt can have many appearances—bold, subtle, light, or dark, all depending on the fabric selections. Choose your favorite look and select your fabrics accordingly. The Baby Boy palette would make a great shower gift. Trade the blues for pinks and call it Baby Girl. The Bumble palette is quite dramatic and is just the right look for Halloween!

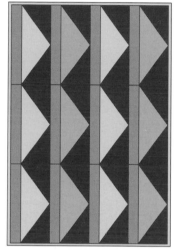

Bumble

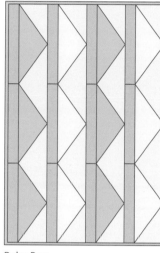

Baby Boy

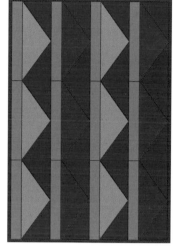

Lipstick

Marmalade

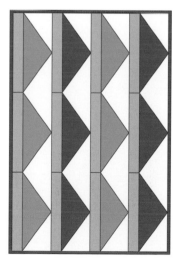

Bottles

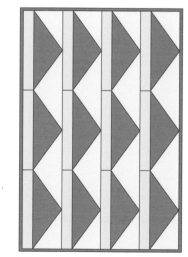

Cosmos

Big Zigzag

Big Zigzag twin-size quilt—Atlantic palette, made by Barbara Cain

Finished quilts:
45″ × 60″ lap size
60″ × 90″ twin size

BIG ZIGZAG IS VERY STRIKING AND FULL OF MOTION. SQUARES AND RECTANGLES COME TOGETHER TO MAKE THIS BOLD AND ACTIVE PATTERN IN SURPRISINGLY LITTLE TIME.

Fabrics

Big Zigzag is made with three colorful fabrics and one neutral background fabric. Solids and prints are both good choices for this design. If you want to use prints, choose nondirectional prints that will blend well at the vertical seam and will read the same whether horizontal or vertical.

The quilt back has a zigzag feature section that is made the same way as the quilt top. Two fabric panels are added to finish off the back. Any type of print will work well for these.

The *Big Zigzag* quilt top featured in this project is made in the Atlantic palette from three solid-color fabrics against a white background. Bright and beachlike, this quilt is ready for an ocean retreat.

Choose your palette for *Big Zigzag* from the Palette Suggestions (page 86). If you would like to create your own palette, keep in mind the role that contrasting fabrics play in allowing the zigzags to stand out.

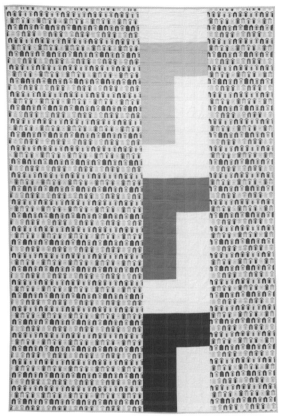

Big Zigzag twin-size quilt back

MATERIALS

Yardages are based on 40″-wide fabric.

Material	Description	Lap quilt (45″ × 60″)	Twin quilt (60″ × 90″)
Fabric 1	Coral solid for the zigzags	⅝ yard	1⅛ yards
Fabric 2	Aqua solid for the zigzags	⅞ yard	1⅛ yards
Fabric 3	Medium blue solid for the zigzags	⅞ yard	1 yard
Fabric 4	White print for the zigzags	1¾ yards	3 yards
Fabric 5	Multicolored print for the back panels	2 yards	4¼ yards*
Fabric 6	Aqua solid for the binding	½ yard	¾ yard
Batting		53″ × 68″	68″ × 98″

* The narrower back panel requires piecing. To avoid piecing, you'll need 5⅝ yards.

CUTTING

Refer to Staying Organized (page 5) for tips on keeping track of your cut fabric.

When subcutting strips, cut the longest pieces first.

Material	Lap quilt (45″ × 60″)	Twin quilt (60″ × 90″)
Fabric 1	Cut 2 strips 8″ × width of fabric; subcut into: 2 squares 8″ × 8″ (1a) 1 rectangle 8″ × 15½″ (1b) 1 rectangle 8″ × 19¼″ (1e)	Cut 4 strips 8″ × width of fabric; subcut into: 6 squares 8″ × 8″ (1a) 1 rectangle 8″ × 15½″ (1b) 3 rectangles 8″ × 23″ (1c) 1 rectangle 8″ × 26¾″ (1f)
Fabric 2	Cut 3 strips 8″ × width of fabric; subcut into: 3 squares 8″ × 8″ (2a) 1 rectangle 8″ × 15½″ (2b) 3 rectangles 8″ × 23″ (2c)	Cut 4 strips 8″ × width of fabric; subcut into: 6 squares 8″ × 8″ (2a) 1 rectangle 8″ × 15½″ (2b) 4 rectangles 8″ × 23″ (2c)
Fabric 3	Cut 3 strips 8″ × width of fabric; subcut into: 4 squares 8″ × 8″ (3a) 2 rectangles 8″ × 23″ (3c) 2 rectangles 8″ × 11¾″ (3d)	Cut 1 strip 8″ × width of fabric; subcut into: 5 squares 8″ × 8″ (3a) Cut 1 strip 23″ × width of fabric; subcut into: 5 rectangles 8″ × 23″ (3c)
Fabric 4	Cut 4 strips 8″ × width of fabric; subcut into: 9 squares 8″ × 8″ (4a) 1 rectangle 8″ × 15½″ (4b) 1 rectangle 8″ × 23″ (4c) 1 rectangle 8″ × 26¾″ (4f) Cut 1 strip 23″ × width of fabric; subcut into: 5 rectangles 8″ × 23″ (4c)	Cut 7 strips 8″ × width of fabric; subcut into: 16 squares 8″ × 8″ (4a) 2 rectangles 8″ × 15½″ (4b) 2 rectangles 8″ × 23″ (4c) 2 rectangles 8″ × 11¾″ (4d) 1 rectangle 8″ × 19¼″ (4e) Cut 2 strips 23″ × width of fabric; subcut into: 10 rectangles 8″ × 23″ (4c)
Fabric 5	Cut 1 piece 26¾″ × 68″ (5g) Cut 1 piece 11¾″ × 68″ (5h)	Cut 1 piece 34¼″ × 98″ (5i) Cut 2 pieces 19¼″ × 49¼″ (5j)*
Fabric 6	Cut 6 strips 2½″ × width of fabric for binding	Cut 9 strips 2½″ × width of fabric for binding

* Carefully cut the fabric so that the print will match when the pieces are joined. OR if you have 5⅝ yards, cut 1 piece 19¼″ × 98″ (5j).

Construction

Big Zigzag is assembled in columns. All seam allowances are ¼″ and are pressed to one side. For odd-numbered columns, press the seams in one direction; for even-numbered columns, press the seams in the opposite direction. Between columns, press all the seams in one direction.

QUILT TOP

Refer to either the lap-size quilt assembly diagram or the twin-size quilt assembly diagram.

1. Sew together the pieces into pairs and press.

2. Sew together the pairs into columns and press.

3. Sew together the columns to assemble the quilt top and press.

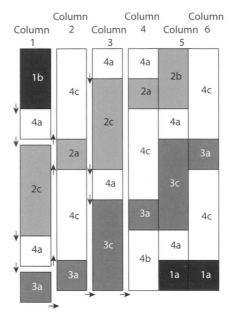

Lap-size quilt top assembly

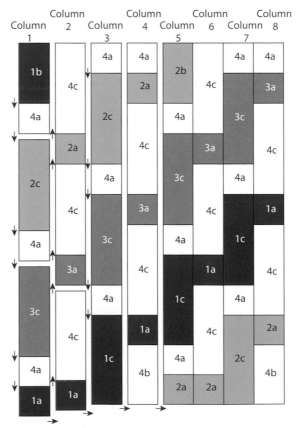

Twin-size quilt top assembly

QUILT BACK

Refer to either the lap-size quilt back assembly diagram or the twin-size quilt back assembly diagram.

1. Sew together the pieces into pairs and press. Note: If you are piecing the back panel for the twin-size quilt, match the print pattern of the 5j pieces.

2. Sew together the pairs into columns and press.

3. Sew together the columns to assemble the quilt back and press.

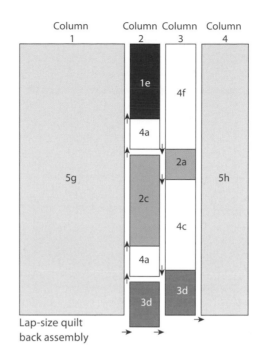

Lap-size quilt back assembly

FINISHING

Refer to Quilt Finishing (page 103) for instructions on sandwiching, basting, quilting, and binding.

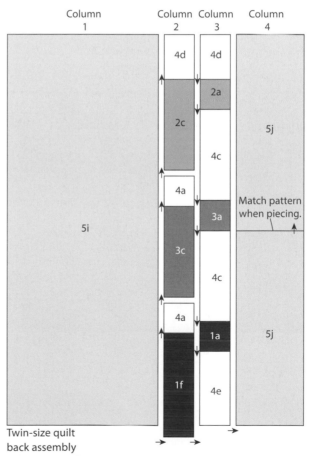

Twin-size quilt back assembly

Palette Suggestions

So much can be done with the *Big Zigzag* pattern. How about refreshing your sunniest room with a Grapefruit zigzag quilt? It will be cool and energizing. The Orchid Ombré palette shows how the zigzag pattern can be made with gradations of one color. Choose your favorite colors and make your zigzags stand out.

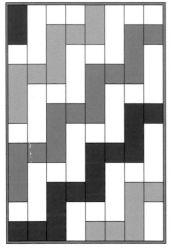

Atlantic

Grapefruit

Charlie

Orchid Ombré

Poppy

Old School

Cutting Diagrams
for Selected Quilts

Big Harlequin
LAP-SIZE QUILT

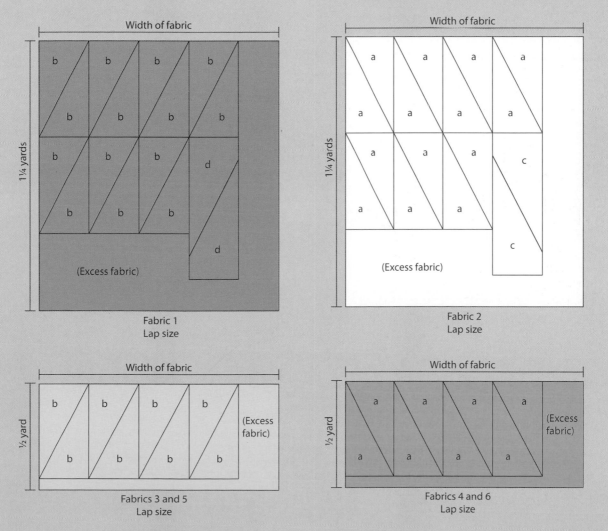

Width of fabric

1¼ yards

b b b b

b b b b

b b b d

b b b

d

(Excess fabric)

Fabric 1
Lap size

Width of fabric

1¼ yards

a a a a

a a a a

a a a c

a a a

c

(Excess fabric)

Fabric 2
Lap size

Width of fabric

½ yard

b b b b

b b b b

(Excess fabric)

Fabrics 3 and 5
Lap size

Width of fabric

½ yard

a a a a

a a a a

(Excess fabric)

Fabrics 4 and 6
Lap size

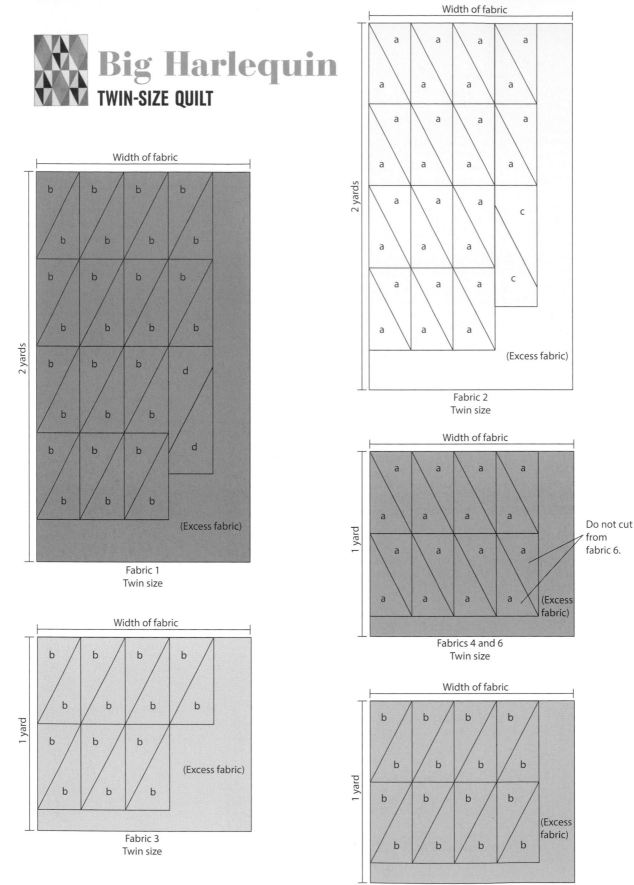

Big Harlequin
TWIN-SIZE QUILT

Width of fabric

2 yards

b b b b
b b b b
b b b b
b b b b
b b b b
b b b b
b b b d
b b b d
b b b
b b b

(Excess fabric)

Fabric 1
Twin size

Width of fabric

2 yards

a a a a
a a a a
a a a a
a a a a
a a a c
a a a
a a a c
a a a

(Excess fabric)

Fabric 2
Twin size

Width of fabric

1 yard

b b b b
b b b b
b b b
b b b

(Excess fabric)

Fabric 3
Twin size

Width of fabric

1 yard

a a a a
a a a a
a a a a
a a a a

Do not cut from fabric 6.

(Excess fabric)

Fabrics 4 and 6
Twin size

Width of fabric

1 yard

b b b b
b b b b
b b b b
b b b b

(Excess fabric)

Fabric 5
Twin size

Big Isosceles
LAP-SIZE QUILT

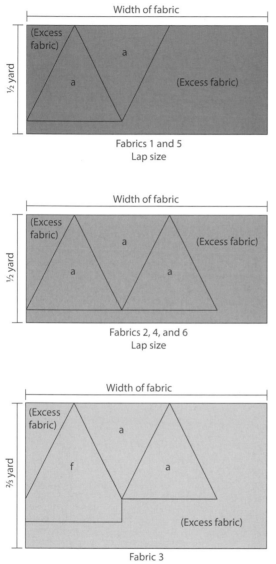

Width of fabric

½ yard

(Excess fabric)

a

a

(Excess fabric)

Fabrics 1 and 5
Lap size

Width of fabric

½ yard

(Excess fabric)

a

a

a

(Excess fabric)

Fabrics 2, 4, and 6
Lap size

Width of fabric

⅔ yard

(Excess fabric)

a

f

a

(Excess fabric)

Fabric 3
Lap size

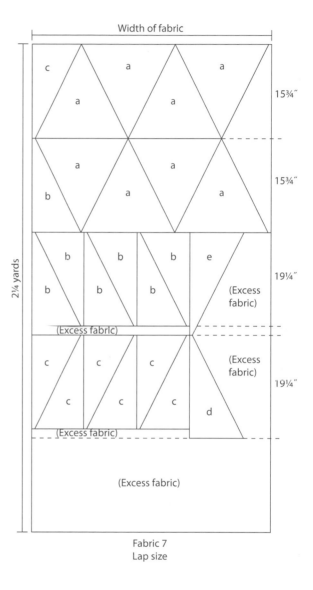

Width of fabric

2¼ yards

c

a

a

a

a

a

a

b

a

a

15¾″

15¾″

b

b

b

e

b

b

b

(Excess fabric)

(Excess fabric)

19¼″

c

c

c

(Excess fabric)

c

c

c

d

19¼″

(Excess fabric)

(Excess fabric)

Fabric 7
Lap size

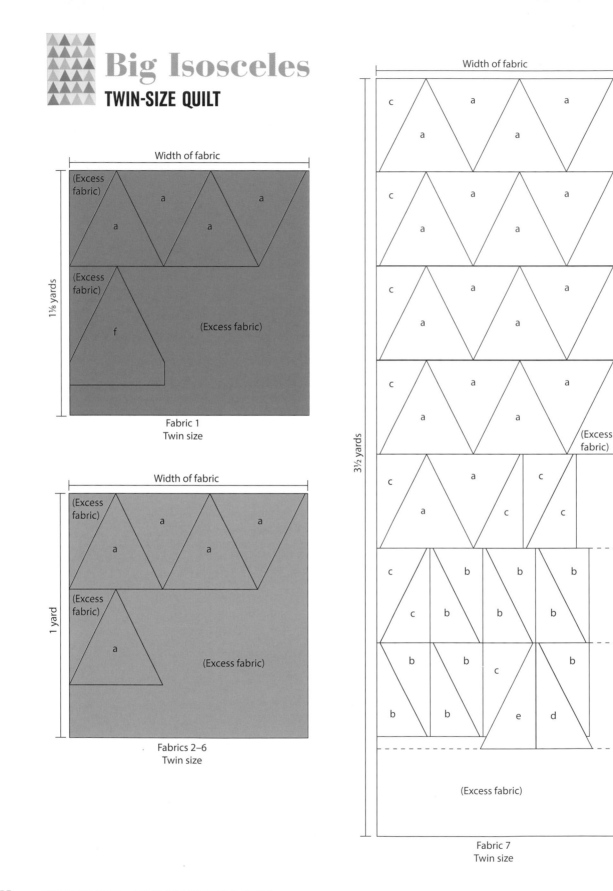

Big Isosceles
TWIN-SIZE QUILT

Width of fabric

(Excess fabric)

a
a

a
a

(Excess fabric)

f

(Excess fabric)

1⅛ yards

Fabric 1
Twin size

Width of fabric

(Excess fabric)

a
a

a
a

(Excess fabric)

a

(Excess fabric)

1 yard

Fabrics 2–6
Twin size

Width of fabric

c
a
a

a
a

15¾″

c
a
a

a
a

15¾″

c
a
a

a
a

15¾″

c
a
a

a
a

(Excess fabric)

15¾″

c
a
a

a
c
c
c

15¾″

c
b
b
b

c
b
b
b

15½″

b
b
c
b

b
b
e
d

19¼″

(Excess fabric)

3½ yards

Fabric 7
Twin size

Big Pennant
LAP-SIZE QUILT

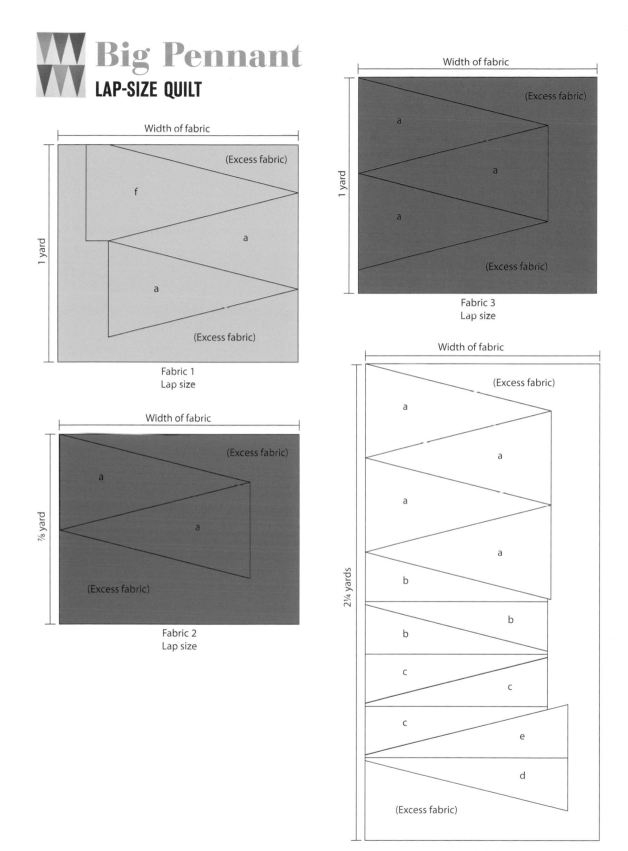

Width of fabric

1 yard

(Excess fabric)

f

a

a

(Excess fabric)

Fabric 1
Lap size

Width of fabric

⅞ yard

a

(Excess fabric)

a

(Excess fabric)

Fabric 2
Lap size

Width of fabric

1 yard

a

(Excess fabric)

a

a

(Excess fabric)

Fabric 3
Lap size

Width of fabric

2¼ yards

a

(Excess fabric)

a

a

a

b

b

b

c

c

c

e

d

(Excess fabric)

Fabric 4
Lap size

Big Pennant

TWIN-SIZE QUILT

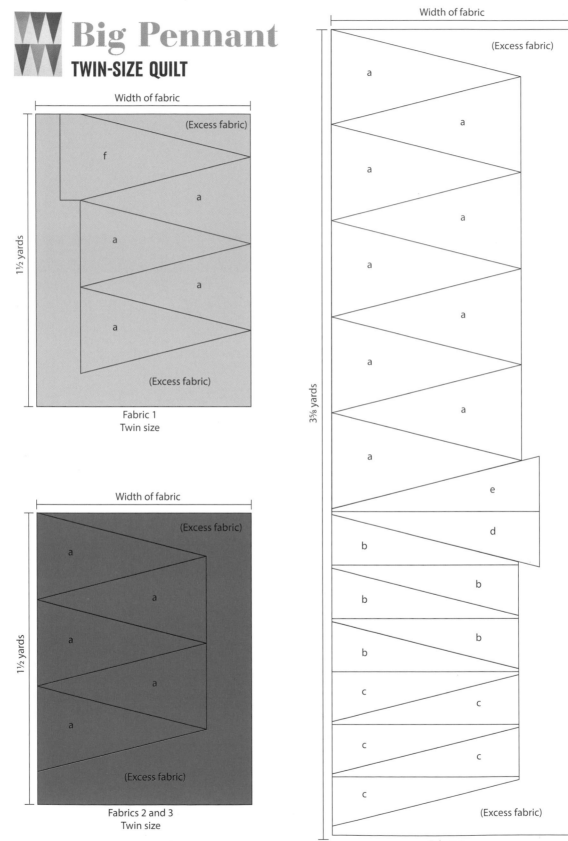

Width of fabric

(Excess fabric)

f

a

a

a

a

1½ yards

(Excess fabric)

Fabric 1
Twin size

Width of fabric

(Excess fabric)

a

a

a

a

a

1½ yards

(Excess fabric)

Fabrics 2 and 3
Twin size

Width of fabric

(Excess fabric)

a
a
a
a
a
a
a
a
a

e
d
b
b
b
b
b
c
c
c
c
c

3⅝ yards

(Excess fabric)

Fabric 4
Twin size

Big Sawtooth

LAP-SIZE QUILT

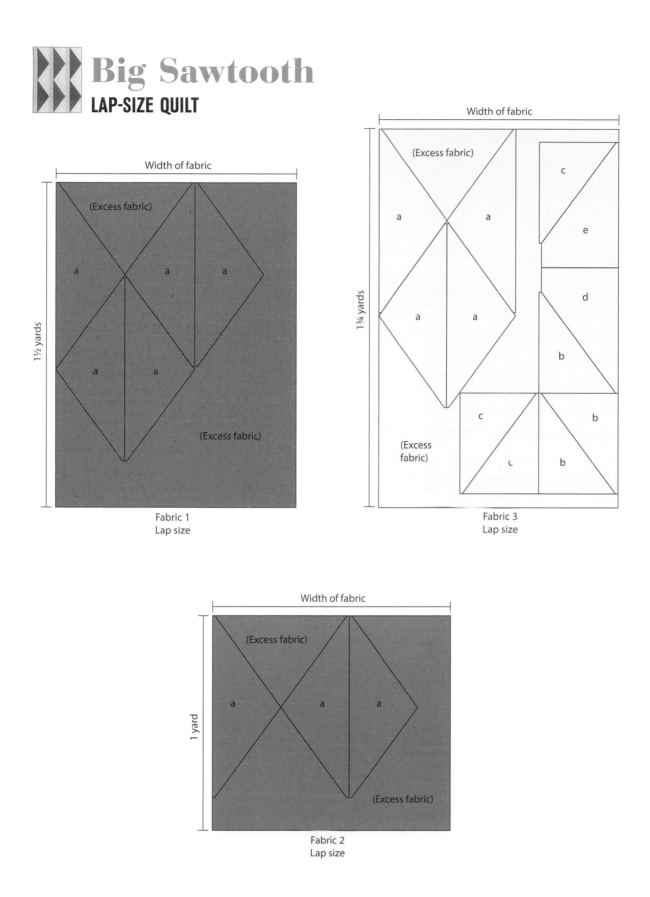

Width of fabric

(Excess fabric)

a   a   a

a   a

(Excess fabric)

1½ yards

Fabric 1
Lap size

Width of fabric

(Excess fabric)

a   a

c

e

a   a

d

1¾ yards

b

c   b

(Excess
fabric)

c   b

Fabric 3
Lap size

Width of fabric

(Excess fabric)

a   a   a

1 yard

(Excess fabric)

Fabric 2
Lap size

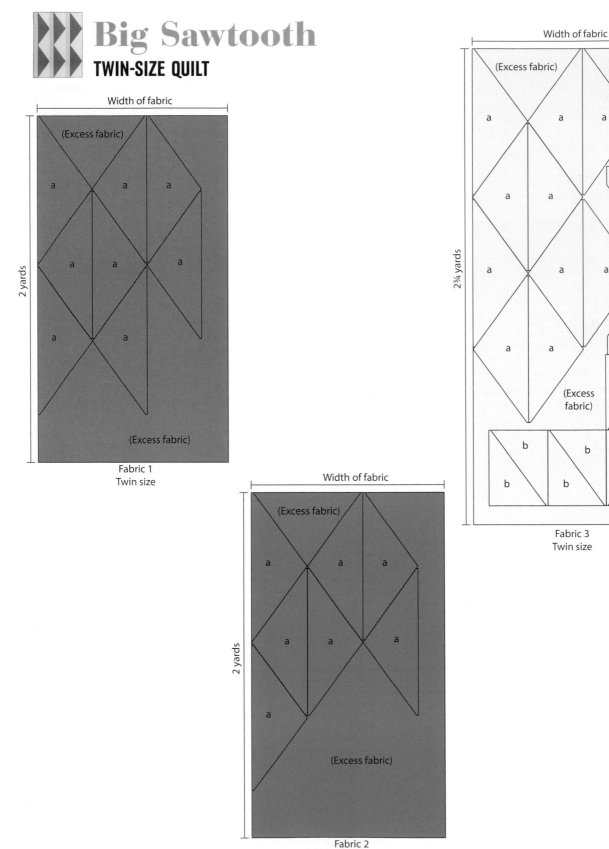

Big Sawtooth
TWIN-SIZE QUILT

Width of fabric

(Excess fabric)

a   a   a

a   a   a

a   a

(Excess fabric)

2 yards

Fabric 1
Twin size

Width of fabric

(Excess fabric)

a   a   a

a   a   a

a

(Excess fabric)

2 yards

Fabric 2
Twin size

Width of fabric

(Excess fabric)

a   a   a

a   a   d

a   a   a

e

a   a

c

(Excess fabric)   c

b   b   c

b   b   c

2¾ yards

Fabric 3
Twin size

Quiltmaking Basics

Materials

Details and recommendations for the materials and tools needed to make the projects in this book are provided in this section.

FABRICS

Yardage	Inches
⅛ yard	4½″
¼ yard	9″
⅓ yard	12″
⅜ yard	13½″
½ yard	18″
⅝ yard	22½″
⅔ yard	24″
¾ yard	27″
⅞ yard	31½″
1 yard	36″

Use good-quality, 100% cotton quilting fabrics. Although most quilt fabrics are sold in 42″–44″ widths, yardages for the projects in this book are based on a usable width of 40″. This is to account for shrinkage, removal of selvages, and for occasional fabrics that are of narrower widths.

Not all retailers sell fabric in eighth-, quarter- and third-yard increments. Depending on where the fabrics are purchased, you may need to round up to the nearest half-yard. The chart provided here will come in handy if you need to round up.

Whether or not to prewash fabric is an age-old debate for which there is no right or wrong answer. It's a matter of personal preference. Prewashing fabric can prevent quilt shrinkage and color bleeding. Conversely, working with crisp, unwashed fabrics is easier and less time consuming than prewashing, drying, and pressing yard goods.

None of the fabrics for the quilts in this book have been prewashed, and due to their good quality, I'm not concerned about future adverse effects. Good-quality fabrics cut, sew, and press well. They also look, feel, and wear better than lower-quality fabrics. Good-quality fabrics also shrink less and bleed less. They do cost more, however. It takes quality time to make a quilt, and the use of quality fabrics will make the effort worthwhile.

Color, Value, Contrast, and Scale

Quilters often think that color is the most important factor when selecting fabrics. While this is true for satisfying a personal preference or for matching a decor, the *value*, *contrast*, and *pattern scale* of the fabrics actually that have the most impact on the appearance of a quilt, as they are what make the quilt design stand out.

You put a great deal of effort into making your quilts, so be sure to make good fabric selections that will enhance your work. By gaining an understanding of value, contrast, and scale, you will maintain the integrity of the design while still using colors that you like.

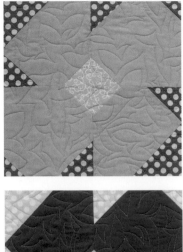

Value is defined as the relative lightness or darkness of a color. "Relative" is the key word. When we characterize colors as light or dark, it is in comparison to other colors/values. In the examples shown here, we consider the same gray fabric to be light in one instance but dark in the other. The medium gray is the darker of the two grays in the block on top. However, the same medium gray is the lighter of the two grays in the bottom block.

Value study

Contrast is another word for difference. Contrasting colors are different colors—for example, red versus blue. Contrasting values are different values, such as light versus dark. The selection and use of contrasting fabrics are critical to making the quilt design stand out. Take a look at the quilt block studies shown here. The block on top is made from two contrasting colors: gray and green, and four contrasting values: dark, dark/medium, medium/light, and light. Note how distinct the block design is. The block on the bottom is made from the same two contrasting colors: gray and green; however, only two values are used: light and medium light. Note how the block design is far less distinct.

Value and color study

Pattern scale is a term used to gauge size—in this case, the size of a fabric's print. Much like value, scale is also relative. A 4″ × 4″ print might be an appropriate scale for a drapery panel, but for a 2″ × 2″ quilt piece, it would be impractically oversized. When selecting prints for a quilt, make selections based on the scale of the print relative to the size of the quilt pieces. The study illustrates how the scale of prints can either enhance or detract from a block design. The block on the top is made with prints that are appropriately scaled, so that the block design remains distinct. The block on the bottom, however, is made with prints that are a bit too large in scale. The fabrics dominate, competing with the shape of the block and detracting from the overall design intent.

It takes awareness, practice, and effort to balance value, color, and scale when choosing fabrics for a quilt. The payoff, however, makes it all worthwhile.

Pattern scale study

BATTING

Most quilt batting is made of cotton or polyester or a blend of the two; however, wool, bamboo, and silk products and blends are also available. Each material has its own characteristics, advantages, and disadvantages. A review and comparison of package labeling or a consultation with a shop owner can help you narrow down your selection.

The projects in this book are made with Warm & Natural needled cotton batting. It is a low-loft, supple batting that will not separate, bunch, or beard (page 108) and can be quilted up to 10˝ apart. This is a critical characteristic, particularly for the larger-scale, open-quilting designs featured on some of the projects in this book.

Whichever batting you choose, it's important to follow the manufacturer's instructions for maximum quilting distances and care.

THREAD

As with fabric and batting, use good-quality thread. High-quality thread breaks less, looks better, and wears longer than poor-quality thread. Your choice between thread made of cotton, polyester, a blend of the two, or an alternate fiber is best made when based on the characteristics that you prefer. If you prefer a matte finish to your thread that will blend in well with the cotton fabric, cotton is likely your best choice. Keep in mind, however, that cotton threads do not have much give and may produce more lint than synthetic threads typically do. If you prefer a high-luster, highly visible thread, synthetic products are for you. As a bonus, they are typically stronger than cotton, produce less lint, and do have some give, which results in fewer thread breaks.

I used three types of thread for the quilts in this book. For the piecing, my choice is Coats & Clark Quilting and Piecing Thread, a low-lint, cotton-covered polyester. Black, gray, white, off-white, and taupe were the only colors needed. Piecing thread is barely seen on a finished quilt, and therefore color matching is not critical.

For machine quilting thread, however, color choice is critical, as these stitches are quite visible. Each project was quilted using a heavier-weight, high-sheen polyester thread that was selected for its color, visibility and durability. I use Floriani 40-weight polyester embroidery thread.

Lastly, for the machine-finished bindings, I used matte cotton thread. Match this thread color with the color of the binding fabric so that it is barely visible.

TOOLS

Binding Clips. After attaching the binding to the front of the quilt, I prefer to use binding clips instead of pins to hold binding in place prior to the final stitching.

Iron. Have a good, basic steam iron on hand.

Ironing Board. Use a padded ironing board measuring at least 54″ long. This will handle an entire width of fabric and will still have room for the iron.

Painter's Tape or T-Pins. When making a quilt sandwich (page 103), use low-tack painter's tape to hold the quilt back in place on a hard surface. If securing the quilt back to a soft surface such as carpeting, use T-pins.

Pencil. Use a pencil to mark light sewing lines on the wrong side of fabric when sewing squares or rectangles using a diagonal seam. The lines will not be seen from the right side and will not bleed when pressed with steam or when washed.

Permanent Marker. Use a fine-point permanent marker, such as a Sharpie or a Pigma Micron pen, when tracing around templates onto fabrics. The lines will be easy to see when cutting, and the marks will not bleed when pressed with steam or when washed.

Pincushion. Keep track of pins by using a pincushion or a magnetic pin tray.

Rotary-Cutting Equipment. Use a 45mm or larger rotary cutter, a self-healing cutting mat, and a 6″ × 24″ gridded rotary ruler.

Safety Pins. Use curved or quilter's safety pins to pin baste a quilt sandwich (page 103).

Scissors. Use good-quality fabric scissors that cut well and that are kind to your hands. The handles should be textured enough to allow you to hold the scissors firmly without using a strong grip, but not so rough that they cause irritation.

Seam Ripper. Keep a seam ripper on hand, as it will be needed.

Sewing Machine. A basic home sewing machine with a good straight stitch is all you will need for piecing. It can also be used for straight-line quilting if fitted with a walking foot (page 110). If the feed dogs (page 109) can be lowered, it can also be used for free-motion quilting when fitted with a darning foot.

Sewing Machine Needles. For machine piecing, use universal needles, size 80/12. For machine quilting, use 90/14 quilting needles.

Spray Starch. Spray starch will stabilize your fabrics before making bias cuts. There are many brands available. Be sure to test the spray on a scrap of fabric first and to wash your quilt after it is quilted and bound.

Straight Pins. Use sharp, thin, steel straight pins to hold fabrics in place while sewing.

Tape Measure. Have a retractable metal tape measure on hand for making large templates and for measuring yardage.

General Techniques

General techniques used in making the projects in this book are explained below.

CUTTING

Cutting fabric with rotary-cutting tools rather than scissors is quicker and more accurate. With rotary tools, several layers of fabric can be cut at one time with neat and accurate results. Rotary cutting also minimizes the need to measure and mark the fabric prior to making the cuts.

Before cutting, press the yardage, and then square it up. To square fabric, fold it in half across its length. Shift the selvage edges against one another until the folded edge drapes evenly without pulling or puckering. When this occurs, the crosswise grain of the fabric is square relative to the selvages.

Fold fabric in half, matching selvage edges.

Shift to even out.

Place the fabric onto a rotary-cutting mat, and align the horizontal marks of the ruler with the folded edge of the fabric.

Using a rotary cutter and ruler, trim the uneven raw edges from the fabric perpendicular to the fold. You now have a straight edge to begin your cuts.

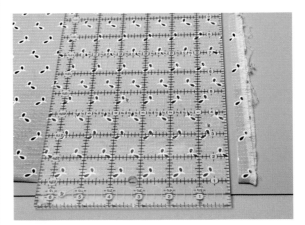

Trim raw edges.

The square- and rectangle-based projects in this book typically call for strips to be cut from the width of fabric and then to be subcut into individual pieces. To cut strips across the width, rotate the cutting mat 180° so that the newly straightened edge is on your left. Align the desired vertical line on your ruler with the straight raw edge and cut strips to the desired width using a rotary cutter.

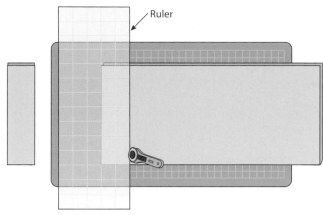

Cut strips to desired width.

To cut squares or rectangles, cut a straight edge on the end of the folded strip, removing the selvages. Rotate the strip and measure from the cut end to subcut squares and rectangles.

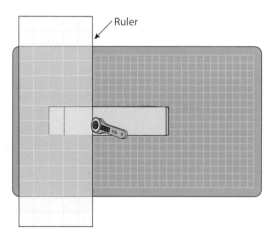

Subcut squares and rectangles.

Safety First

Rotary blades are extremely sharp and must be handled with great care. When using a rotary cutter, use an acrylic ruler designed for rotary cutting and a rotary-cutting mat. Cut away from your body and ensure that your hands and fingers are away from the ruler's edge. Close the blade when not in use. Dispose of used blades either in the case in which they came or by taping them between two sheets of cardboard and placing them in the trash.

PIECING

Use a ¼″ seam allowance for all projects in this book. Sewing an accurate ¼″ is critical to successful piecing. There are several ways to set up your machine for ¼″ seams.

- Use a ¼″ presser foot. If your machine did not come with one, you can purchase one.

- Use a seam guide, such as the fast2sew Ultimate Seam Guide from C&T Publishing.

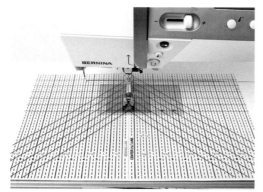

fast2sew Ultimate Seam Guide

- Adjust your sewing machine needle so that you can use the edge of a standard presser foot as a guide. Do this only with a zigzag throat plate.

For pieced units to come out the correct size, you will need to sew what is called a "scant ¼″" because the thread and the fold of the fabric take up a bit of space. Sew a scant ¼″ by sewing just a thread or two shy of the ¼″ mark.

Check Your Piecing Accuracy

An easy way to check your accuracy is to cut 2 pieces of fabric that are exactly 2½″ wide. Sew them together with your ¼″ seam and then press the seams to one side. The pressed piece should measure exactly 4½″. If it doesn't, make adjustments until you get the precise results needed.

PRESSING

Press with care so as not to stretch and distort the shape of fabrics and cut pieces. Use an up-and-down motion as opposed to moving the iron back and forth across the fabric. If you have stubborn wrinkles, use a quick shot of steam when pressing down. The up-and-down motion is particularly important when working with bias edges, as they are extremely vulnerable to stretching. Pressing fabrics with spray starch before cutting bias pieces will also help maintain their shapes.

Where seams intersect with other seams, press seam allowances in opposite directions to distribute the bulk of the fabric throughout the intersection. Pressing directions are included with the project instructions.

Quilt Finishing

After the top and back are pieced, prepare for machine quilting by making a quilt sandwich and basting the layers together. Quilting by machine allows you to finish quickly and enjoy your quilt sooner.

MAKING A QUILT SANDWICH

1. With a permanent marker, make a small tick mark at the exact center of each of the four sides of the quilt back, batting, and quilt top.

2. On a large, flat, hard surface, spread the quilt back wrong side up and tape down the edges with painter's tape, keeping the marks exposed. If you prefer to work on carpet, secure the backing to the carpeting with T-pins.

3. Center the batting on top of the backing, smoothing out folds and wrinkles. Match the marks along the sides to ensure that it is centered.

4. Center the quilt top right side up on top of the batting and backing, again using the marks as a guide.

BASTING

Baste the sandwich together by using curved or quilter's safety pins placed approximately 3″–4″ apart. Begin pinning in the center and move toward the edges first in vertical columns and then in horizontal rows. If possible, avoid pinning on intended quilting lines. Remove the securing painter's tape or T-pins.

QUILTING

Choose either straight-line or free-motion quilting patterns to enhance the design of the quilt. A small sampling of easy but effective designs is provided here, although the possibilities are endless. Refer to the batting manufacturer's recommendations for maximum distances between quilting lines. Remove the basting pins as you progress. Refer to Resources (page 111) for books on machine quilting.

Straight-Line Quilting Patterns

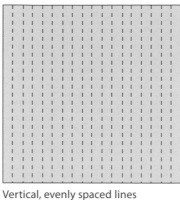
Vertical, evenly spaced lines

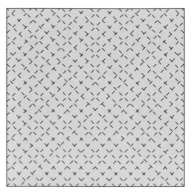
Diagonal crosshatch

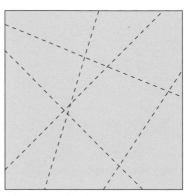
Grid or crosshatch

Random parallel lines

Diagonal lines

Random straight lines

Free-Motion Quilting Patterns

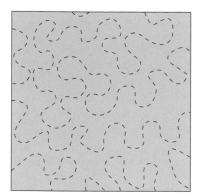

Meander

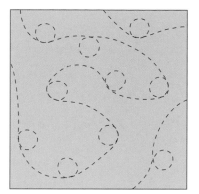

Loops

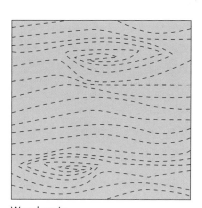

Wood grain

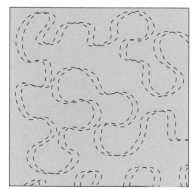

Ribbon

Mixed loops

Topographic

TRIMMING

Trim the excess quilt backing and batting, aligning all the edges with the quilt top. Use a square ruler at the corners of the quilt to ensure that they are 90° angles.

BINDING

Binding is the final step in completing your quilt. I use a double-fold binding made from strips that are cut 2½″ wide for all of my quilts.

Make Double-Fold Binding

1. With right sides together, place 2 binding strips perpendicular to one another and sew diagonally from corner to corner. Trim the seam allowance to ¼″ and press open. Repeat the process until all of the strips are sewn together.

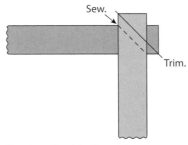

Sew together binding strips.

Diagonal seam

2. With wrong sides together, press the entire strip in half lengthwise.

Sew Binding to Quilt

- -

Tip

To avoid having a binding seam land on a corner, preview where the seams will land by placing the binding around the quilt. If a seam lands on a corner, shift the starting point and try again.

- -

1. With raw edges even, pin the binding end to the front edge of the quilt, several inches away from a corner. Leaving the first several inches of the binding unattached, begin sewing the binding onto the quilt using a ¼″ seam allowance.

2. Stop sewing ¼″ away from the first corner and backstitch 1 stitch.

Stop sewing ¼″ from corner.

3. Lift the presser foot and raise the needle. Rotate the quilt one-quarter turn. Fold the binding at a right angle so it extends straight above the quilt and the fold forms a 45° angle in the corner.

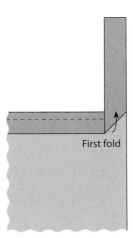

Fold up binding.

4. Fold the binding strip down, even with the edge of the quilt. Begin sewing at the folded edge.

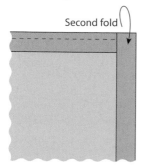

Make second fold and continue sewing.

5. Continue sewing around the quilt, repeating Steps 2–4 at each corner.

6. When you are several inches away from the beginning of the binding strip, stop sewing and remove the quilt from the machine.

7. Fold back the ending tail of the binding strip on itself where it meets the beginning tail. From the fold, measure and mark the cut width of the binding strip, which in this case is 2½″. Cut the ending binding tail to this measurement.

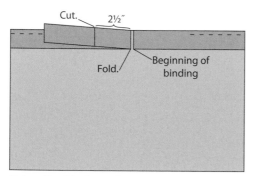

Cut ending binding tail.

8. Open both tails. Place one tail on top of the other tail at right angles, right sides together. Mark a diagonal line from corner to corner and sew the tails together on the line. Take a quick peek to ensure that the tails are correctly connected and that the binding fits correctly. If not, adjust accordingly. Trim the seam allowance to ¼″. Press open.

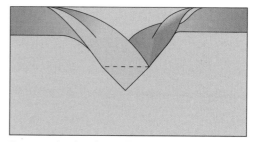

Sew together binding tails.

9. Refold the binding and finish sewing the binding to the quilt.

Finishing the Binding

1. Fold the binding over the raw edges to the quilt back so that it covers the stitching line.

2. Using binding clips, temporarily secure the binding in place around the entire perimeter of the quilt.

3. Sew the binding down by hand on the back, mitering the corners as you encounter them. If you prefer, you can machine stitch-in-the-ditch (page 109) from the front.

Glossary

Backing

Backing, or quilt back, is the layer of fabric that is on the back of a quilt. A quilt usually consists of three layers: a top, batting, and backing. A backing can be a single cut of fabric or a pieced design. In this book, the backings are all pieced so that the quilts are reversible.

Basting

Basting is the method by which the layers of a quilt are temporarily held together to keep them from shifting when quilting. Basting can be done by hand sewing, pinning, tacking, or spraying with a light basting adhesive.

Batting

Batting is the padded layer that is in the middle of a quilt. Most quilt batting is made of cotton or polyester or a blend of the two. However, wool, bamboo, and silk products and blends are also available.

Bearding

Bearding is the undesirable fuzz that appears over time on a quilt's outer surface. It is the result of fibers migrating from the batting layer through the top or backing. Bearding is mostly associated with inexpensive polyester products, although it can also occur with wool and silk batting.

Bias

The bias is the diagonal direction across the surface of a woven fabric. Fabric cut on the bias is vulnerable to stretching and must be handled with care.

Binding

Binding is the long, thin strip, or connected strips, of fabric that covers the raw edges of a quilt. Binding can be cut on the crosswise grain or on the bias and is usually double folded for durability. Bias bindings are particularly flexible and are useful on quilts with curved edges.

Block

Blocks are a basic building unit of many quilts. They are usually square or rectangular in shape and are typically combined with other blocks to make a quilt.

Chain Piecing

Chain piecing is the method by which fabrics are sewn together, one set after another, without stopping to clip apart the connecting threads until after a chain of sets is formed. It may also be called *assembly-line piecing*.

Column

A column is a vertical arrangement of quilt pieces and an assembly method for some of the quilts in this book.

Crosswise Grain

Crosswise grain is the direction of woven fabric that runs perpendicular to the selvages. Crosswise threads and cuts have more stretch to them than straight grain (parallel to the selvages). Crosswise threads are also referred to as the *weft*.

Darning Foot

A darning foot is a sewing machine attachment that is used with lowered feed dogs to enable free-motion quilting. This allows the quilter to move fabric freely in any direction while sewing.

Directional Prints

Directional prints are printed fabrics that have a clear direction to them. The direction can be one way or two way. One-way prints look correct only when oriented in one direction. Two-way prints look the same whether they are oriented in one direction or in the opposite direction.

Ditch

The ditch refers to the seamline of a quilt. Stitching-in-the-ditch is sewing or quilting directly in the seamline. This type of quilting is very unobtrusive.

Domestic Machine Quilting

Domestic machine quilting is quilting with a typical home sewing machine.

Feed Dogs

Feed dogs are the teeth located under the presser foot of a sewing machine that move the fabric while sewing. During free-motion quilting, lowering the feed dogs allows the fabric to move freely in any direction.

Finished Size

Finished size is the completed dimension of a block or quilt. It does not include seam allowances.

Free-Motion Quilting

Free-motion quilting is the method of quilting in a fluid, continuous motion with lowered machine feed dogs and a darning foot.

Grain

Grain is the direction of threads in a woven fabric, consisting of straight grain and crosswise grain, which are also referred to as the warp and weft, respectively.

Length of Fabric

The length of fabric is the span that runs parallel to the selvages.

Loft

Loft is a gauge for describing the thickness of quilt batting. High-loft batting is thicker and fluffier than low-loft batting.

Longarm Machine Quilting

Longarm machine quilting is done on a specialized machine that has a long arm. The quilter moves the machine rather than the fabric. Most longarm machines are equipped with a stationary frame to which the quilt sandwich is attached and held tautly while the machine is maneuvered when sewing.

Matching Points

Matching points is ensuring that the corners and peaks of quilt pieces match either one another or an adjacent seamline without being over or under extended.

Miter

A miter is a join that occurs at a 45° angle.

Nondirectional prints

Nondirectional prints are printed fabrics that have no clear direction to them. The nondirection can be tossed or four way. Tossed prints look correct in any direction. Four-way prints look the same in any 90° orientation.

Palette

A palette is the selection of colors used in a particular quilt.

Quilting Foot or ¼″ Foot

A quilting foot is a domestic sewing machine attachment that measures a precise ¼″ from the needle to the outer edge of the foot.

Raw Edge

A raw edge is the cut, unsewn edge of a piece of fabric or a quilt assembly.

Right Side

The right side of fabric is the printed or front side of a piece of fabric.

Row

A row is a horizontal arrangement of quilt pieces.

Sandpaper Board

A sandpaper board is a sturdy board covered with superfine-grit sandpaper. It prevents fabrics from shifting when marking stitching lines and seam allowances.

Sandwich or Quilt Sandwich

A sandwich is a stacked quilt assembly consisting of three layers: top, batting, and backing.

Seam Allowance

A seam allowance is the distance between the sewn seam and the raw edge of the fabric.

Selvage

Selvages are the tightly woven outer edges of a fabric.

Straight Grain

Straight grain is the direction of woven fabric that runs parallel to the selvages. Straight-grain threads and cuts have less stretch to them than crossgrain. Straight-grain threads are also referred to as the warp.

Subcut

A subcut is the second cutting of a piece of fabric, usually a strip, into smaller pieces.

Template

A template is a shape cut from a heavy, rigid material that is used as a pattern for making multiple units of the same shape.

Unfinished Size

Unfinished size is the dimension of a block or other quilt assembly including the seam allowances.

Value

Value is a gauge for describing how close a color is to either white or black in terms of lightness or darkness.

Walking Foot

A walking foot is a domestic sewing machine attachment that helps feed the top layer of a quilt sandwich evenly with the backing layer that the feed dogs pull.

Width of Fabric

The width of fabric is the span that runs from selvage to selvage.

Wrong Side

The wrong side of fabric is the unprinted or back side of a piece of fabric.

About the Author

When Barbara was a young girl, her mother taught her how to sew clothing. After she understood garment making, Barbara's interests quickly turned to home goods. She began making kitchen linens, decorative pillows, bedding, and, most important, quilts! Barbara had an undying interest in all things textile—so much so, that she pursued an education in interior design. This was followed by a long career as a partner of an architectural firm, where she honed her design skills.

Due to the demands of her occupation, quilting had been a luxury hobby, as Barbara's free time was very limited. It was because of this that she recognized her need to continue making quilts but without making a huge time commitment. This need resulted in the development and writing of *Go Big, Go Bold—Large-Scale Modern Quilts*, where Barbara shares her expertise in creating large-scale, sizable quilts with rewarding speed.

Follow Barbara on her blog modernquiltingbyb.com.

Resources

FABRIC

I use fabric from the following manufacturers. The listed websites provide information on the fabrics available and where to buy them.

Andover Fabrics
andoverfabrics.com

Michael Miller Fabrics
michaelmillerfabrics.com

Riley Blake Designs
rileyblakedesigns.com

Robert Kaufman Fabrics
robertkaufman.com

Westminster Fibers /
Lifestyle Fabrics
westminsterfabrics.com

ONLINE FABRIC RETAILERS

Hawthorne Threads
hawthornethreads.com

Hancock's of Paducah
hancocks-paducah.com

Fat Quarter Shop
fatquartershop.com

BATTING

I use batting from The Warm Company for my quilts. Their website provides product information and where to buy them.

The Warm Company
warmcompany.com

THREAD

I use thread from the following manufacturers. The listed websites provide information on the products available and where to buy them.

Coats & Clark
coatsandclark.com

Floriani Embroidery Sewing
& Quilting Products
florianisoftware.com

ONLINE RESOURCES

For instruction and inspiration, I use many of the popular online resources such as YouTube, Flickr, Instagram, and Pinterest. An online resource that you might not be familiar with is design-seeds.com. It provides wonderful color and palette inspiration—I highly recommend that you take a look.

QUILTING BOOKS AND OTHER PRODUCTS FROM C&T PUBLISHING

Books

Beginner's Guide to Free-Motion Quilting by Natalia Bonner

First Steps to Free-Motion Quilting by Christina Cameli

Foolproof Machine Quilting by Mary Mashuta

One Line at a Time, Encore by Charlotte Warr Andersen

Other Products

fast2sew Ultimate Seam Guide by Annis Clapp

Inchie Ruler Tape (repositionable adhesive measuring strips to perfectly align machine-quilting designs)

Essential Sandboard from Piece O' Cake Designs